Just Pursuit

A Black Prosecutor's
Fight for Fairness

Laura Coates

Simon & Schuster

New York   London   Toronto   Sydney   New Delhi

While the stories in this book are based on my experiences, names, locations, and identifying details have been changed. Conversations and dialogue in the book are based solely on my recollection and are not intended to represent verbatim transcripts.

Simon & Schuster
1230 Avenue of the Americas
New York, NY 10020

Copyright © 2022 by Laura Coates

First Simon & Schuster hardcover edition January 2022

SIMON & SCHUSTER and colophon are registered trademarks of Simon & Schuster, Inc.

For information about special discounts for bulk purchases, please contact Simon & Schuster Special Sales at 1-866-506-1949 or business@simonandschuster.com.

The Simon & Schuster Speakers Bureau can bring authors to your live event. For more information or to book an event, contact the Simon & Schuster Speakers Bureau at 1-866-248-3049 or visit our website at www.simonspeakers.com.

Interior design by Lewelin Polanco

Manufactured in the United States of America

1 3 5 7 9 10 8 6 4 2

Library of Congress Cataloging-in-Publication Data
Names: Coates, Laura Gayle, author.
Title: Just pursuit : a black prosecutor's fight for fairness / Laura Coates.
Description: New York : Simon & Schuster, [2022]
Identifiers: LCCN 2021041619 (print) | LCCN 2021041620 (ebook) |
ISBN 9781982173760 (hardcover) | ISBN 9781982173784 (ebook)
Subjects: LCSH: Coates, Laura Gayle. | African American public prosecutors--United States--Biography. | Discrimination in criminal justice administration--United States.
Classification: LCC KF373.C585 A3 2022 (print) | LCC KF373.C585 (ebook) |
DDC 340.092 [B]--dc23/eng/20211004
LC record available at https://lccn.loc.gov/2021041619
LC ebook record available at https://lccn.loc.gov/2021041620

ISBN 978-1-9821-7376-0
ISBN 978-1-9821-7378-4 (ebook)

To my children, Adrian and Sydney.
If you are never more than you are today,
to me you were always enough.

Contents

CONTENTS

CONTENTS

Just Pursuit

Introduction

The pursuit of justice creates injustice.

Before I became a prosecutor, I never imagined that could be true. I thought that the job would be an uncomplicated act of patriotism and that justice was what happened when a person was fairly tried and convicted for their crime.

For years, I stood inside a courtroom, representing the people of the United States. I witnessed firsthand how our just pursuits caused collateral damage in ways I couldn't have imagined when I answered my calling to leave private practice as a civil litigator and join the Department of Justice.

My time at Justice began as a trial attorney in its Civil Rights Division. As a child, I knew the stories of Ruby Bridges and the Freedom Riders better than the tales of Dr. Seuss. My mother grew up in a segregated North Carolina, only migrating north when her parents found work—her mother as a domestic worker and her father, a butler and chauffeur—for some of the wealthiest White families in the Northeast. These families were the namesake of industry leaders—companies that I later happened to represent while working for large law firms. My father spent most of his childhood in foster care, and, although he was raised in a relatively integrated Massachusetts, he was still a Black boy in 1950s America.

In spite of their humble beginnings, my parents propelled themselves to becoming among the first generation in their families to not only go to college but also earn advanced degrees. My parents' paths crossed in western Massachusetts, when they were students at neighboring Smith and Amherst Colleges, each only one of a relative handful of Black students at their respective schools. They met just two years after Reverend Martin Luther King Jr. was assassinated, when the fight for equality was far from over. They spoke often of the housing discrimination they had experienced while raising my two older sisters and me, and I watched the economic struggles faced by my father while trying to build a dental practice in a country where financing eluded Black people. While laws were in place, the nation's conviction for equity never seemed to catch up. I was taught to understand the civil rights era not as finite but as a movement that we were all duty-bound to keep in motion.

Joining the Civil Rights Division in their work to enforce the Voting Rights Act was in service of that duty. The pride I felt working for the DOJ was immeasurable, but the bureaucracy was unbearable. Unsurprisingly, lobbyists and elected officials at the state and federal levels were particularly interested in our voting rights work, and would often interfere, rendering an investigation futile. I needed a reprieve from the paperwork. I thought being in trial would help, but federal trials in the enforcement of voting rights were few and far between.

One of my Black colleagues told me about a program he had participated in early in his career that allowed DOJ attorneys with few trial opportunities to go on temporary detail to a U.S. Attorney's office in Washington, D.C. He always spoke so glowingly about his experience, regaling me with hilarious stories of courtroom antics and theatrics. My request to participate was repeatedly denied, however, since the program wasn't readily available to voting rights lawyers, so I applied to work at the United States Attorney's office directly.

When I received my offer, I headed to my colleague's office for his congratulations. Instead, his normally jovial mood darkened when I told him that it was not a temporary six-month detail but a permanent position with a four-year commitment.

He closed the door, saying, "Two words, Coates: human misery." He counted each word on his fingers. "I don't know how to describe it other than to say that you're not going to be able to get used to that type of human misery every day. There is nothing you can really do about it either. It just keeps coming."

I was shocked. As a prosecutor, I assumed he would have been the only one in the courtroom who actually *could* have done something about the misery. Isn't that what was meant by justice?

"Look, all I can tell you is be careful. You gotta protect yourself. You're better off staying here at Main Justice," he said, distinguishing our work from that of United States Attorneys across the country. "It's a lot to deal with."

I felt apprehensive as I watched him close his eyes in remembrance. But I wasn't leaving the Department of Justice, I told myself, just working in a different capacity. I assumed it would be similar enough and that my work as a federal prosecutor in a criminal courtroom would be held in the same high regard as my work within the Civil Rights Division. I chalked up his admonishment to an assumption that he lacked what I clearly believed I had: fortitude.

In fact, the transition from enforcing civil rights legislation to criminal prosecution represented a seismic shift in how others perceived me, and even how I perceived myself. I had been a trusted champion of people who looked like me. But now, I was often distrusted as an agent of a system that disproportionately filled prisons with people who looked like me.

This created a struggle, an internal battle of allegiance, between the competing facets of my identity. It wasn't always clear which should win. For seven years, I upheld my oath as a public servant, but my work put me at odds with my principles and lived experience as a Black woman.

Over this time, I prosecuted in the name of justice while injustice unfolded on the national stage. I gave birth to my son the year Trayvon Martin was killed. I nursed my son while watching Trayvon's mother fight for justice for her own. As the country debated whether Trayvon had been racially profiled by a wannabe cop, I consoled myself with the fact that I was in a position to punish a real one who might profile another woman's child. Then I had my daughter. Three months later, Michael Brown was killed. I followed the case and saw the way the grand jury process was used to undermine the potential prosecution of the police officer who had shot Brown. As the country vilified the prosecutor's decision not to indict the officer, I told myself that I was different from that prosecutor. As a Black woman and mother, I believed that I would never exploit the power I had over a grand jury to somehow deny justice. I convinced myself that I needed to remain a prosecutor to balance the system. And then Tamir Rice was killed. And I heard the familiar script of officers attempting to justify their use of force. The same script used by officers testifying against defendants in my own cases. And I looked at my growing son, who always tracked at the highest percentiles of height, and was terrified that he may one day be the little boy mistaken for a man.

And then I looked at my husband, a Black man who now feared his own death at the hands of police officers. He would ask me to explain why it was so hard to charge the officers in these cases.

"There's no recourse? How can that be? Isn't there some way . . ."

My answers could never alleviate his fear, only explain the

process by which I had been trained. I again tried to distinguish myself, assuring him that prosecutors like me would make different decisions. But a part of him was resigned to the possibility that I might be the exception and not the rule. I was terrified that he was right, or worse, that I had fooled myself into thinking I could actually be the exception.

We wondered how soon to have "the talk" and not the one White people have with their kids. We needed to teach our children how to interact with police officers, and refused to let either of them play with toys that even slightly resembled a weapon. I knew it wasn't fair to limit my children this way, but I didn't know how not to be afraid.

And then came the day my husband stopped asking me questions about prosecutors' charging decisions and instead installed a camera in our car. I laughed, thinking that he had purchased another unnecessary gadget for himself. His expression dissolved my smile. He told me that the camera was for me. If he were ever killed by a police officer in a traffic stop, he just wanted me to know what happened. He had heard me talk so often about the rehearsed scripts officers used to justify their excessive use of force, he hoped this would be a way to capture the truth. It was his love letter to me, and it broke my heart.

As an insider, I felt powerless to ensure justice. I eventually became distrustful of a system in which I was a decision maker. I looked around the courtroom through the eyes of a prosecutor, but also as a Black woman, daughter, sister, wife, and mother. I couldn't stomach the homogeneity of the defendants inside the gate compared to the people outside of it. Out of the hundreds of criminal matters I prosecuted in court, I can count the number of White defendants I saw on one hand.

The imbalance was revolting. I cringed at how accustomed the courtroom had become to a choreographed routine, with everyone knowing their place and role. Two armed marshals wearing rubber gloves would stand behind the defendants, waiting for the judge to nod—a command to restrain them. As natural as it was for me to clasp my hands together in front of my body, so it was for the defendants to hold their hands behind their backs without prompting, expecting to feel the metal of handcuffs.

I questioned my own role within the system. Others did too. Black defendants would pass me with an air of surprise that I was standing where they assumed a White man would be. My allegiance was also on trial. Was it to the laws of the United States? To the Black community? To the officers? To the powers that be? These constituencies were increasingly at odds. When I first became a prosecutor, I had thought each case could represent a dot on the arc that Dr. King hoped would bend toward justice. Now, I wondered if I was bending the arc of justice or breaking it, and afraid the justice system might just break me.

I was no longer confident that my presence in the system was an asset and not somehow a betrayal. Even guilty verdicts couldn't prevent collateral damage to the victims. I knew these stories needed to be told, but my position as prosecutor served to muzzle me. I debated whether to leave my job, unsure whether I could make a bigger impact as a participant or a spectator of the justice system.

After four years, four words revealed the clear choice. I was standing in the hallway of the courthouse after having won yet another trial, securing yet another guilty verdict against yet another Black person. My White supervisor had watched my closing argument and had accompanied me for the verdict. He was showering me with praise as he held his hand up for a high five. My hand met his.

"We got another one!" he exclaimed, wrapping his hand around my flat palm and pumping it in the air. Before I could respond, he walked away, disappearing into another courtroom to watch another colleague's trial. I didn't need to meet the eyes of another Black person standing in the hallway to know that my own should have been lowered.

I replayed that moment for days, turning the phrase over in my head.

"We . . . got . . . another . . . one!"

My entire being recoiled. I tried not to project my own feelings on my supervisor and extend the benefit of the doubt, but his words felt like an indoctrination. For my conscience, it was the proverbial final straw. I walked away the day my four-year commitment ended, not knowing whether I had been a proud champion or a coward, complicit or exonerated, the public's humble servant or its slave. What I did know was that one day my children would realize that I was only human, and I needed to be able to look them in their eyes when they did.

I wanted them to know what it meant to pursue justice, and what could happen along the way to the people with the power and to those who are powerless. I gave birth to my two children while a prosecutor, and I wanted them to understand the thoughts I carried within me as I carried them into the world. I wanted that world to be just. I removed the muzzle and used my experiences in the courtroom as a guide to educate the public as a law professor, news analyst, and radio talk show host. In that, I have found a new calling.

When I left the job, I left the files on my desk, but I took the memories with me in the hopes that by sharing the injustices I'd witnessed, justice itself might one day be possible. What follows are those stories.

1

Please Don't Come Here

*On What Happens When a Black Woman
Must Aid in a Deportation Arrest*

Prosecuting a car thief is light work for a federal prosecutor, particularly when the thief is eventually captured after a high-speed chase. Which is what happened in a case with a relatively young defendant, Shawn, who was already notorious in the police department. To describe Shawn as a menace would be like calling bubonic plague a cold. His total disregard for the law was heightened by the fact that he had consistently evaded conviction on technicalities. An uncontrollable, unearned ego had replaced his common sense. This time, the office wanted to ensure there would be no technicality.

It all began when Manuel, a middle-aged Latino man, went out to get his car, only to discover it had been stolen. He was cooperative with the police and with the prior assigned prosecutor during pretrial discussions in spite of his reluctance to participate in the process. I had only just inherited this case right before trial, and expected for the victim's testimony to be short and sweet. He wasn't in the car when it was stolen. He hadn't seen the defendant. All that was required was that he testify that he was the lawful owner of the vehicle and hadn't authorized the defendant to use the vehicle for any purpose. That was it.

9

As is customary, I ran a criminal background check on all witnesses I intended to call at trial, and on the victim. When I ran Manuel's, I was surprised to see a warrant for immediate deportation appear in the results. He had been captured illegally crossing the southern border and ordered to report to a detention facility. That was twenty years ago, when he was sixteen years old. The previous assigned prosecutor apparently never bothered to check.

Since then, he had been law-abiding and had led a quiet life in the United States. He was gainfully employed and had a driver's license—something you can obtain without having citizenship. While his immigration status was irrelevant in a criminal prosecution, I was required to alert the federal marshals before he could take the stand if the warrant was active. I nervously checked to see whether the warrant was indeed active. It was. I repeated the word "no" in my head and stared at the screen, my eyes darting back and forth as I figured out what to do next. This man could get deported after twenty years because his car was stolen by some young jerk?

With the trial two days away, I sought advice from my supervisors. Surely there was a precedent for immigration issues in an international community like Washington, D.C.? There wasn't. The nature of the warrant was irrelevant; we were required to turn the person in to the appropriate authority regardless. Could I warn him first? Sure, if I wanted to lose my law license. I reached out to the victim liaison, who told me to call and tell him not to show up to trial and not to report his whereabouts to the marshals. If anyone asked, she said she'd take the heat, in the hopes I wouldn't be disbarred. But did I really intend to go down for a woman who had just introduced herself during that same phone call? Instead, I asked my supervisors to consider dismissing the charge. They declined. Another technicality was unacceptable for this defendant.

I ran it up the chain and tried to get a meeting with the powers that be. At the very least, I hoped to appeal to the fear of a public relations debacle. I refreshed my email neurotically waiting for a response. Sleep was not even a thought. It was just before 5:00 on the morning of trial before I got my final directive, a phone call from a high-level supervisor who had the final say: "You are not to dismiss the case. You know the location of a twenty-year fugitive. Report his location immediately to ICE."

"Do we have a liaison with ICE? Is there a lawyer or someone we could talk to so I am not just reporting him to an arrest-hungry ICE agent? There's gotta be some way—" I pushed back.

"Is there something you didn't understand? I'm happy to have someone else handle this for you if you are incapable of fulfilling your professional obligation." The threat was hardly veiled.

"No, sir, I'll handle it myself."

I was at the office by 5:30 a.m., researching case law and victims' rights. I had already tried consulting with ethics personnel, searching for any way to avoid the inevitable. I knew it was in vain. The second I saw him in the courthouse, I would have to alert the marshals about his warrant. Not only would they arrest him before he was able to take the stand, it would all but guarantee an acquittal. The thought of the defendant's freedom in exchange for the victim's detention was hard to bear. I waited outside the U.S. Attorney's office, hoping that I could get a meeting. No one was in yet, and no one answered my calls.

I didn't bother to pray that he wouldn't show up. If that happened, I would be required to request a material witness warrant for the arrest of a subpoenaed victim who failed to appear at trial. Just in case I had any idea of turning a blind eye to the absence, the managing supervisor had specifically instructed me to request the warrant in our early call.

It was quickly approaching 8:00 a.m. and we were due to be

in court in less than two hours when I was notified that the victim was waiting for me downstairs in the lobby. He had misread the subpoena and thought he was supposed to come to my office rather than go straight to the courthouse. His mistake had bought me more time and him a chance.

I begged for the words to come to me as I rode the elevator down. I thought about what my colleagues had advised. One closed the door behind him before he told me, "Tell him to run, Coates. You're a Black woman. Fuck the office. I couldn't have that on my conscience."

Another had told me not even to bother to meet him. "Let immigration deal with him. It's not like he's coming with clean hands in this. He shouldn't have called the police when he knew he had an immigration problem."

Still another said, "Turn him in. It will make you look good to the office."

And finally: "I would've kept my mouth shut. It's not your job to help execute warrants. We've got too much on our plate already."

None of the response felt right. I regretted soliciting their opinions, knowing each ear I bent could become a loose lip.

As I walked out to greet the man, I realized that the only picture I had ever seen of him was the one taken in connection with his detention twenty years ago. I searched the lobby and, spotting a man who resembled Manuel's younger self, held out my hand. He was professionally dressed, wearing a suit. His shoes had just been shined. He smiled and nervously shook my hand. "How are you?" he asked.

"I'm fine, sir. I'm trying to figure out something. I wasn't expecting to see you here. Do you mind waiting for me for a second? If I just had some more time. Well, can you wait?"

"Yes, no problem." And with that, he took a seat.

The head of security stopped the elevator with his hand as it started to close behind me.

"Ms. Coates, right?" he said.

"Yes."

"I understand that there is an individual here today with an active warrant. Is that right?"

"Yes," I said, as my shoulders dropped.

"I'll take care of it. You don't have to be involved."

"Wait." My voice cracked. "What does that mean? What do you mean you'll take care of it? Don't just cart him away. He has rights, doesn't he? Did you already call ICE?"

"I intend to contact them now. Don't worry, this doesn't need to concern you."

"But I just shook that man's hand. He's waiting for me. He'll think it's a trap. I just need to make sure there's no other way. I have until the courthouse, don't I?"

"No," he said kindly. "Look, this isn't going to be easy for you."

"I'm not exactly worried about myself. He's wearing a wedding ring. Who will tell his wife? Look, I'll call ICE. But I'm assuming you're going to watch me do that, huh?"

He smiled and followed me upstairs to my office to prevent a scene in the main lobby of the building. He already knew the way.

I called ICE and asked them a transparent hypothetical. I explained that I had a victim in a criminal case who might have a deportation warrant. Was there any exception for this instance? No. The warrant was active and they were en route. Already? How much time did I have? Twenty-five minutes.

I frantically called my supervisors again. Nothing more could be done. I was told to go to the courthouse. Someone else would handle the transfer of the suspect.

The head of security remained in my office and assured me that he would let me speak to the ICE agents before they arrested the victim. It would prevent a scene if I could walk him to a private area, the guard explained. He didn't want to spook already reluctant people waiting in the lobby by having someone inexplicably arrested in their presence.

We sat in silence in my office while he waited for notification that the agents had arrived. When the call came, he ushered me down the hallway, stopping one last time to say, "Last chance. You really don't have to do this. Security can escort him to the guards for you."

"No," I replied, as we walked into the elevator. "It's my fault this is happening. I'll tell him personally. I don't know what he has in front of him. Hey, did he, are you sure he's still here? Maybe he left on his own?" The guard didn't bother to answer. We both knew he would not have been permitted to leave the building for any reason. We rode downstairs in silence.

As we got off the elevator, my direct supervisor was waiting to board. She saw my face and let the elevator pass, waiting to speak to me in the hall instead. She asked for the status. I informed her of the early call with another supervisor and told her that ICE was on their way and that I was going to escort the victim personally. She set down her bags and stood beside me to check my emotional temperature. She asked if I wanted her to come with me. I declined, fearing that the crowd would further intimidate the victim. As we spoke, the U.S. Attorney exited an elevator, smiling at me, and then asked me how my day was going. My supervisor explained that I was about to turn in a man with an active immigration warrant to waiting ICE agents. He simply asked, "This isn't something we did, right?" I explained that the warrant had pinged during a background check and that I had been ordered to report the issue, as is our policy with every active warrant.

He asked, "Do I need to be here for this?" My supervisor advised against his direct involvement, citing a publicity issue.

"Is there anything we can do, sir?" I asked.

"We all have to make tough decisions." And with that, the U.S. Attorney turned away and retreated into the safety of the elevator. My supervisor pushed the elevator button to head to her office, while I proceeded to speak with the waiting ICE agents. They introduced themselves. One was Black. The other appeared to be Latino. I asked them what was going to happen. One flirtatiously looked me up and down, smiled at me, and said not to worry my "pretty little self" about it, and that he'd "take care of me." I told him to fuck off, and turned to the other one, ready to spread my dissatisfaction. I was in no mood to entertain anyone's antics. He explained the situation and said that the man would be handcuffed. He motioned to a nearby van with its engine idling. I asked if his family would be notified.

"Yes. Usually, eventually. Sometimes after."

"After what?"

"Sometimes they can't be reached until after deportation." I shuddered at the thought of that first phone call home and the helplessness his family would feel.

There was no time to pivot. Their demeanor changed to impatience. I walked back to the lobby. I asked the security guard who had been acting as my de facto chaperone to wait with the agents so I could speak with Manuel privately, but he politely refused. He couldn't accommodate that request. I asked my chaperone whether he spoke Spanish. I hoped he did not, so that I could speak freely. He didn't. I approached Manuel for a second time. This time, to the surprise of my chaperone, I greeted him in Spanish.

I motioned toward my chaperone. My expression was grave as I explained, "Sir, we don't have much time together. I'm very sorry, but when you entered the building, security discovered your deportation warrant. Immigration officials are here to arrest you. I've been trying to stop it, but I can't. This man next to me isn't going to let you leave. Prepare yourself. Please understand that I couldn't warn you."

He stood up and looked at the exit at the same time a security guard assumed his position beside the door.

He began to breathe heavily and looked frantically around.

"It won't happen here, sir. It will be in private so you won't be embarrassed. I'm very sorry this is happening," I explained in Spanish.

His feet robotically complied and he walked beside me into a private area. Selfishly, I wanted to beg for his forgiveness. I needed to be absolved of any guilt for the role I had played in the realization of his nightmare. But I didn't dare ask for that luxury. I had not mistaken myself for the victim. His knees buckled as the ICE agents placed his hands behind his back. The same agent who had promised to take care of my pretty little self jokingly pulled on his arms and said, "Ándale, cowboy," while Manuel tried futilely to regain his footing. I continued to speak in Spanish to him and told him that he had rights, that I wasn't sure but I assumed they would be required to provide him counsel, so he should ask for a lawyer immediately. Explaining that he might not have a chance to call someone from there, I asked him for the password on his phone so I could contact his family now. He gave it to me and told me to call his wife, his boss, and his pastor. I tried to hold the phone to his ear while he listened to the ringing, but his knees continued to buckle.

The agents had had enough and tried to place him in the van. I protested, shouting that I outranked them in clearance and position. Aware this was nothing but a feeble power flex, I was desperate to find some way to remind them that he still had rights. In an instant I had morphed into his personal attorney intent on vindicating those rights. At the very least, I wanted to contact his family and secure counsel. I didn't know if I was entitled to do any of that, but I didn't care. A moral obligation credentialed my authority.

Manuel began to urinate on himself as his chest heaved. I saw the stain form, and turned to the agents to request bathroom access. They said that there would be a bathroom at the detention facility. I stood in front of Manuel, hoping to block their view in an attempt to give him some form of dignity. I tried his wife again. This time she answered. I held the phone to his ear again while he said, "I've been caught. I love you." A heart-wrenching wail leaped from the phone as he was ushered away. I stayed on the phone and told her who I was and what had happened, and I gave her my information. She cried hysterically, repeating the question, "Where will they take him?" I wrote down her phone number, told her I'd contact their pastor, and advised her to get a lawyer. I also said that he would be okay. But I knew that was a lie. I started to cry but stopped myself. I had no right to cry in front of this man. I surrendered his phone to the agent's expectant hand.

My chaperone exhaled loudly as he watched the ICE agent tuck Manuel's head into the van. We watched the van as it drove away. He was still watching the empty parking space when he said, "I've never had to do that before."

I asked if he was okay.

"No," he said. "You?"

"No," I said. "It feels like the worst day of my life."

"I imagine that he'll win that contest, Laura." Of course he was right.

When that man's knees were buckling under the weight of the knowledge that he would be deported, he didn't try to run. He didn't beg. He tried to stand like a man. He simply asked me to call his wife, his pastor, and his boss—to let him know that he wouldn't be able to work today. God, love, and country, right? In all the ways that mattered, I had led an American away that day.

I walked to my supervisor's office, closed the door, sat down, and cried. I hardly knew her then. I told her to please not judge me for crying. I knew it made me look weak and ridiculous.

She chuckled. "Frankly, I'd judge you if you weren't crying."

She sat beside me, without judgment, and held my hand until the crying stopped. "You did the right thing. You had no choice," she said. "Why didn't you let security handle it?"

"Because I'm not a coward," I said.

With that, she opened her door and said, "I know. Time for trial, right? You're already thirty minutes late. I already let the judge know you're on your way."

I walked into the courtroom and was immediately chastised by the judge for my tardiness. *Doesn't the government have a clock? Do you think you're above the law? If you were a defendant, you'd be in a cellblock if you exhibited such disregard for the court's calendar.* I listened with my hands folded in front of me, trying to stand under the weight of shame. I cleared my throat and said, "Your Honor, you're absolutely right. I ask the court to extend me a professional courtesy and allow me to approach the bench with the defendant's consulting counsel."

Given my reputation, it was clear that this request, along with my tardiness, was out of character, and the judge indulged me, if only out of sheer curiosity. The judge put on the husher, a white noise sound effect used to prevent eavesdropping at the bench, and covered the microphone with his hand. My voice broke as I spoke.

"Your Honor, I'm sorry, but I don't actually know what to do right now. I've just had to turn over my victim to ICE for immediate deportation. I—I'm not sure how long they will hold him or whether the length of time in this country or the fact that he has children will allow him to remain here and under what circumstances. If I could—if I could just have a moment to think. The courtroom is full today and I just need a moment to collect myself."

I expected the judge and the defense counsel to exchange eye rolls and berate me for having the audacity to request a moment of silence. Instead, the judge leaned in and told me to watch him closely but to disregard his words and his actions for the next two minutes. Defense counsel nodded and winked quickly at me. With that, the judge began to point at his watch and the clock on the wall, fiercely and dramatically pointing at me while he muttered about the weather, the news of the day, and his breakfast. I only caught a few words, but I never took my eyes off him, as instructed. At the end of his performance, he turned off the husher and played to the audience. "Have you heard enough?"

I calmly responded, "Yes, thank you, Your Honor."

My eyes and head were clear. I turned on my heels and stood behind the counsel table, ready to put it all on the record.

"As I explained at the bench, my witness may have an outstanding immigration issue that has rendered him unavailable. The length of that unavailability is presently unknown, but I expect to have additional insight by the end of the week. The government asks for a brief continuance to resolve the issue. In the alternative, the government is prepared to go forward on the remaining charges that do not require that victim's testimony, but intends to re-bring the dismissed charge at a later time."

The defendant agreed to the continuance to avoid two trials. The only available date was a month away. I didn't know if I'd even have a victim by then or what might happen to him.

As I returned to my office building, I ran into two Black male prosecutors, who asked me how it had gone. I fought back tears and only managed to shake my head to convey "not now." Like emotional bodyguards, they escorted me to my office, deflecting attention from me as colleagues passed by. When we reached my office, I told them the story. Their reaction was silent but visceral. I could see my own emotions on their faces: first sadness, then resignation, then resistance. Out of a collective feeling of helplessness, we prayed for Manuel. They left as I checked the ICE detainee locator website to see where they had placed him. I called his wife, his pastor, and his boss and gave what information I had.

I continued to check the ICE detainee locator website, incessantly, hoping to find confirmation of his release or his detention. Three days later, the system indicated that he had been released. I was contacted by his attorney, asking whether our office would assist him in securing a U visa. U visas are for immigrants, including undocumented immigrants, who are the victims of certain serious crimes and who have cooperated with authorities in the prosecution of the perpetrator. I inquired, but the powers that be refused to help him, because they didn't feel that the crime he was the victim of was violent or serious enough to warrant a U visa. Surprisingly, even after my office refused to help him in that way, he still cooperated with the prosecution.

The next time I saw him was at the courthouse on the new trial date. He was flanked by a victim advocate whom I had worked with many times. Manuel refused to speak to me in English. My Spanish vocabulary failed me as I searched for the words to ask how he was doing and to apologize once again for the situation. He turned away from me and stared at his bilingual advocate. I asked for her assistance in explaining that there were some unanticipated delays and a request from the defendant to postpone the trial date again. She refused. "You should have requested an interpreter, Laura. That's not my job. As you remember, he needs an advocate for a reason."

I addressed him directly. "Sir, it is my understanding that you are bilingual, but I see that you would prefer not to speak to me in English right now."

So I switched back to Spanish. And then I turned to the advocate and expressed my disappointment in her for her refusal to act as an effective liaison. "It's disappointing and counterproductive."

She scoffed. "He's the one who should be disappointed with you. He never thought the enemy would look like you."

He nodded in assent. He saw me as the enemy, a cruel embodiment of a law he could not change, and he treated me accordingly. I looked at him and took note of his contempt for me. I tried to allow his attitude toward me to assuage my guilt, to use it as an excuse to distance myself from the case and distinguish the parts we were both forced to play. I couldn't. And I tried to leverage whatever remaining power I had in the moment to correct the injustice I couldn't forgive. In a last-ditch effort to give Manuel a chance to get counsel and convince the judge to allow him to remain in the jurisdiction at the very least until the case was fully resolved, I didn't press for an early trial date, and the case was postponed several months out. By the time it reached trial, I had been promoted to another section and the case was reassigned to a different prosecutor. This non-coward didn't fight to keep the trial. The defendant was easily convicted by my successor. Ironically, while his appeal was pending, the victim's deportation was too.

That's not the person I thought I was. I always thought, if confronted with justification for civil disobedience, I would act on my principles, not on a directive. Yes, Manuel had crossed the border illegally, but it was cruel to treat him more criminally than the defendant who was actually on trial. Manuel's own crime was comparatively benign, but he was also the victim of a serious crime. The former should not have negated the latter.

21

Yet my directive subordinated his own victimization. Anxiety-ridden or not, I followed that directive. In a way, I felt like I was no better than a test subject in the infamous Milgram experiment who knew the consequences of her actions but subjugated her protest to her decision to follow an order. I justified my cowardice by telling myself that it was my duty as a prosecutor to carry out the order I was given. I understood the gravity of carrying out the order. I had a choice to warn him, not to inform the marshals, not to call ICE. I had the choice to take a chance and suffer the personal and potential professional consequence of disbarment for my disobedience. I had a choice, and I chose to follow orders. That's not the person I thought I was.

After all, how could I, a Black woman, do that to another person of color in this country? How could I have a hand in oppression? Had I been *just* a prosecutor, I would never have wrestled with the issue. Manuel had illegally crossed the border and ignored a court order. Wasn't that enough to diminish my professional compassion? But instead, there are many descriptors that precede my hyphenated America. A Black woman. A wife. A mother. A public servant. A human being. But the law, no matter how unjust the consequence, came first that day. And in spite of my office's lauding me a patriot and unflappable professional, I will question that choice for the rest of my life.

2

Wanna See Something Funny?

*On Being Trained by a White Male Colleague
How to Interrogate a Black Defendant*

"Let me show you how it's done, Coates. It's gonna give you a high."

Holden, a fellow prosecutor, had graced my door repeatedly in the months since I had begun working at the office. He was only a year older than me chronologically but two years my senior at the office and relished the chance to impart his presumed wisdom. For him, training a peer was the ultimate feather in one's cap, an opportunity to establish oneself at the helm of the hierarchy. But it wasn't just professional strategy; it was psychological ambition. He desperately wanted to be that guy. That guy with whom everyone was friends. That guy who everyone said knew everything. That guy who was always within six degrees of separation from the latest gossip. That guy whom you wanted to show you the ropes. That guy you couldn't wait to tell a story to just to get his reaction. No one ever told him he wasn't any of those guys.

I was in my first trial rotation, after a stint arguing appeals. Leadership wanted prosecutors to rotate through different sections of the office so that they would understand a cross section of the law. It was ideal to begin in the appellate section so that you could vicariously experience the trial mistakes that could lead to an overturned conviction and avoid them in the courtroom. It was now my first week in a trial section, and I was trying to remember those mistakes as I meticulously combed through the files preparing for multiple trials that were within days of one another. I considered calling the prosecutor from whom I had inherited these cases, each of which presented its own Pandora's box. I wanted to rage not only about his lack of consideration for scheduling three back-to-back trials within a two-week period but also for his leaving each case in a unique state of disrepair. I knew that complaining to him would be an exercise in futility—the trials would go on as scheduled and I would make it work—but I needed to make clear that I was not one to be hazed. People must be taught how to treat you, and those lessons are transferable.

I was reaching for the phone to give that lesson when Holden popped his head into my office and dangled a carrot of distraction. In the moment, his offer to help stood in stark contrast to the cavalier approach of my predecessor—and I bit. In a world where baptism by fire is the standard, willing mentors with free time are few and far between. When one offers their time, you leap at the chance to be led through a rite of passage. So I leapt.

I followed my colleague, who seemed perpetually tickled by defendants. We wandered into the basement, navigating a labyrinth of cement corridors with a series of locked doors shielding occupants from view. It was eerily reminiscent of an asylum.

"Where are we going?" I said expectantly, with an attempt at levity.

"We're going to question a witness. See what he says."

"Witness to what?"

"You'll see . . . oh, and, um, a few things to keep in mind. You gotta learn to speak their language. Get 'em to think of you as a friend. You're just like him and he's just like you—only much dumber. Watch how I maintain control. This is psychological warfare. You've got to go in with the right mindset. You ever been down here before?" He didn't wait for my answer.

I hadn't.

"This is where people come when they can't just walk through the front door," he said, with an exaggerated gravitas that sounded rehearsed.

He paused at a door with a guard standing outside. "Showtime," he declared with a smile.

I paused for a moment, hesitant to pass the threshold yet curious to see the spectacle he seemed intent on showing.

A young Black defendant sat clutching the restraints around his wrists. The sound of rattling chains echoed in the tiny room as he tried to adjust his legs to sit up higher in his chair. I watched as he fidgeted with his hands and quickly adjusted his body to brace himself for whatever was coming, shifting his focus from me to Holden. He quickly glanced over his shoulder, confirming his proximity to the wall and looking back at his attorney, who was talking on his cell phone. The attorney acknowledged our presence only with a faint lift of his chin.

The defendant leaned away from the table, placing his hands in his lap as Holden slid the remaining chair from the table, leaving me standing. I casually leaned against the wall to avoid seeming like an awkward sidekick.

Oblivious to the dynamic, Holden crossed his leg, locked his fingers, clasped his hands together over his knee, and reared back in his chair. He nodded a few times, smirking, not saying a word, before saying: "'Sup, *may-un!*" He extended his arms out to his sides like a man greeting an old friend.

I'd never heard my White colleague say that before. His tone was so obviously mocking that my lips and the young man's curled back in unison, as if we had smelled the same repugnant stench.

"You want my chair?" the young man asked me, ignoring Holden.

"This one's chivalrous, huh? Think he likes you, huh?" Holden jeered.

"No, thank you"—I threw a disgusted glance toward my colleague—"I'll grab a chair from outside."

Not to be shown up, Holden swiftly rose to his feet to retrieve a chair from the hallway. As he approached the door, he reached toward me, lightly patting my forearm, and said, "Don't worry, this one won't hurt you."

The chained defendant and I simultaneously scoffed; it was the second time our reactions mirrored each other.

The attorney held up two fingers, pulsing them in my direction to indicate he'd be done with his call in just a few minutes. Holden opened the door and leaned his upper body out of the doorway, peering around the hallway in search of a chair. The bottom of his shoe lifted in the air. He squawked at a guard to slide a chair over from down the hall.

The officer joked about being on break. He made no attempt to retrieve the chair.

Holden pulled his body back through the door, tapped his toe on the cement, pointed his thumb in the direction of the officer, and smirked. "This guy. I'll be right back."

He slid just outside the doorframe, eager to engage the guard. I turned my head to watch his interaction, wondering if his frenetic energy would stop. Each tried to be funnier than the other, trading insignificant barbs. I listened as their punch lines and laughter became more pronounced, more obnoxious, more dismissive of the fact that there was a chained human being here who surely saw no humor in his own situation. Someone's child was waiting for Holden to speak to him.

The only evidence that Holden had not forgotten the people still waiting inside the room was his polished shoe. He used it as a door-stop, ensuring that the door remained open. Each time it began to close he would adjust his foot, giving the impression that he would return any moment to the subject at hand. Each second dragged us into a well of awkward discomfort as I tried not to stare at the young man. He was looking down at the table in front of him, chewing on his bottom lip. I found my distraction in an insistent tapping sound. I scanned the room for the source, my gaze darting from Holden's shoe to the defense lawyer's to the wall vents as I tried to reconcile the volume of the sound with its frequency. I turned to the young man, suddenly aware of his knees shaking, beating against the underside of the table.

"Are you okay?" I asked, realizing that I had no idea why he was even in the building, let alone in those chains.

Just seven minutes before, I had been sitting at my desk when Holden had walked past my office holding a file, asking, "You wanna see something funny?"

I had been eager for a break, after hours of combing through horrible images of unstitchable flesh wounds and trying to compensate for my predecessor's shortcomings. I hadn't even asked Holden for a hint of what we were going to do as he'd shoved away from the door-frame, biting his lower lip as he smiled. He had an elvish quality; he held his mouth as if he were always on the brink of letting you in on a secret, rolling his jaw as he mulled the perfect moment to tell you.

He was the guy who loved an inside joke even if he was the butt of it. An "attaboy" from the right person seemed to be his lifelong ambition—a testament to his relevance. He always had a story to tell, and I had been so eager for a mental reprieve that I'd hastily closed the long manila folder I had been looking through, slicing my finger on the metal tab at the top as I tried to toss it aside for emphasis.

I'd winced, examining my finger to see if I needed a Band-Aid, and noticed blood emerging at the slice. I held out my index finger to avoid getting blood on my clothes as I grabbed my suit jacket from the back of my chair and hastily put it on.

"Hang on. I just gave myself a paper cut!" I'd opened one desk drawer after another, searching for a Band-Aid as the stinging set in.

"Come on!" he'd said, tapping his fingers on the walls like he was playing a keyboard. "Is it really that bad? It's a paper cut, right? Come on! Fix your ouchie later!"

I'd rushed out to him in the hallway, lifting my cut finger as the blood seeped. Grabbing a tissue from the paralegal's nearby desk, I'd walked behind him, wrapping the tissue around my finger before replacing my hair outside of my jacket collar and adjusting my lapels. I'd squeezed the finger to stop the bleeding quickly.

"You good?" he'd asked, looking at the bloody tissue.

"Yeah, it'll stop in a second. Let me just stop in the bathroom really quick and wash my hands."

"No time—we gotta get there. I only have a small window. It's fine. Not like you have to touch anything."

He had almost trotted toward the elevator, turning around once to walk backward to urge me to quicken my pace. He'd repeatedly pushed the button like a child.

He was giddy, and I, intrigued.

"I told you I'd train you. You're gonna thank me for this one."

"This must be good, then," I'd said, giggling at his giddiness.

Seven minutes later, here I was, as expectant and nervous as the person chained before me, self-conscious about what I didn't know or what would be asked of me.

"What'd you say?" the young man asked, bringing me back to the moment.

"I asked if you were alright," I repeated, raising my voice. I slid the tissue off my hand, balling it up into my other hand.

He lifted his hands and showed me his chains, covering his teeth with pursed lips, and raised his eyebrows with derision.

His hands lingered for emphasis before he said, "This how I'm doing." His mouth fell open and he breathed through it.

"What's your name?" I asked.

"Josiah."

"I'm Laura," I said, and instinctively extended my right hand.

He paused for a second before extending his. I lifted my cut finger away from the handshake. He furrowed his brow at the strange grip. I addressed it: "I just gave myself a paper cut. I didn't want to touch you with it."

His hand was cold, clammy, his fingers calloused. Our handshake was weighed down by the shackles gripping his wrist.

He didn't meet my eyes, just stared at my grip, allowing me to scan his face and person unabashedly. Up close, it was clear he was a child who wouldn't see two decades for at least another year. I'd be surprised if he was even eighteen. He seemed timid, eager to release my hand.

"I see you two have met." Holden had returned. He slid a chair through the door and positioned it next to Josiah at the table.

Josiah immediately recoiled, his hands in loose fists, pressed into his hip joints.

"What do you want?" he asked Holden, attempting to conceal his anxiety with annoyance.

"You know what it is, bruh," Holden responded, with the absurd affect of a prep school kid emulating a movie caricature.

"No. I don't know what it is, 'bruh,'" Josiah responded, looking to me for some clarity.

"Really, bruh?" Holden repeated, verbally poking at him.

I dropped my head to one shoulder, shaking it and closing my eyes in an attempt to hide my irritation.

"Give me the folder, Holden. You're wasting everyone's time with this," I offered through a sigh, reaching for the file Holden had placed on the table. I wondered if it were the actual file or something he was using as a kind of prop.

Holden didn't appreciate my impatience and shot an angry glance in my direction as I perused the file. I returned his glance with a raised eyebrow. I leaned back in my chair, opening the file only slightly to shield the full contents from the view of his attorney. I was right about Josiah's age: nineteen. His arrest record was minimal. A couple of dismissed misdemeanor charges, now a felony arrest for drug and gun charges. He was being held in jail until his trial. So why was he in the basement, chained to a chair? I unsuccessfully searched the file for an answer, waiting for Holden to exhaust his newfound vernacular.

That's when I came across a directive in the file: he was a potential informant. No pleas were to be offered without the explicit consent of the higher-ups. It wasn't clear what he knew, only that he "might know something about it."

"You know your brother Cee, right?" Holden asked Josiah. "I want to know who Cee was really shooting at."

"My brother's not Cee," Josiah said, jerking his head back away from his chest in surprise.

"Oh, you don't know Cee?" Holden demanded.

"No. That's not my brother's name."

"Oh, now he's not your brother. You don't know Cee? You don't know Cee." Holden got increasingly irritated, laughing at Josiah between statements as he continued his repetition.

"No. I don't know Cee," Josiah answered, searching my face for an explanation. I didn't have one.

"You want to fuck with me about this?" Holden exclaimed, kicking his chair back from the table, a cringeworthy act that produced the sound of metal scraping against concrete. He'd obviously seen this in a movie. "You don't know Cee. Is that what the fuck you're saying?"

Josiah's attorney looked up from his phone but didn't move.

I wondered if the guard outside was concerned at all about the loud noise.

"I'm not fuckin' with you," he said, incredulous. "I don't know Cee. Who are you talking about?"

I expected Josiah's attorney to interject, to tell Holden to back off and calm down. The sophomoric display of the foaming-at-the-mouth cop played like high school theater to me. But his lawyer was still on the phone, pressing his fingertips against the base of it as if it were a landline and he could prevent the person on the other line from hearing the entire conversation, while he followed what was unfolding before him.

I held up my palms and pointed to the lawyer's phone, gesturing at the absurdity of his still being on a call. The attorney mouthed the words "I know . . . " and pointed his index finger to signal he would just be a minute—then rolled it in the air to indicate that we should keep going, as he pointed to his ear to let me know he was still listening to us.

Impatient, I held up my hand mid-air, yo-yoing it in front of Holden, urging him to ease up. It was as productive and frustrating as an Abbott and Costello routine, with Holden unrelenting. "Really. You don't know your own fucking brother? Come on, man."

"I don't have a brother named Cee," Josiah scoffed.

"Well, what's your brother's name, then?"

Josiah paused, cautious not to implicate or arouse suspicion inadvertently.

"Yeah, that's what I thought. So he is your fucking brother."

"No . . . that's not my brother's name. I only have one brother, and he's dead. He didn't even live around here. I don't know any-one named that."

Holden motioned to Josiah's attorney with his hand. With a glance, the attorney confirmed that Cee was indeed not his client's brother.

I wondered if this was the funny part Holden had teased in my office—the part where the prosecutor got the wrong intel and would concoct a way to save face.

Instead, Holden flicked his index finger under his nose and sniffed. He let out an exaggerated sigh of concern and took the file from my hands, flipping a page over the back of the folder. He paused at a blank fax cover sheet and pretended to read from it. He whistled, feigning exasperation. "I wanted to offer a plea, but you're not telling me anything. We can't help you."

The word "we" caught both Josiah and me off guard.

"Look, Josiah," I offered, realizing that my presence alone may have made this my case too. "I'm not going to shout at you or try to tell you your family tree. But you're facing a serious felony charge, and the man next to you is supposed to be helping you get out of it. As you can see, he's on the phone. Which, frankly, I don't un-derstand why he thinks is okay." The attorney squinted at me—I seemed to have insulted him—and looked at Holden. I tried an-other question. "Do you know why you're here, Josiah?"

"No. They just told me they were bringing me over to speak to someone about my case."

"Did they tell you what we wanted to speak to you about?" I continued, hoping his answers would demystify this encounter. He was as in the dark as I was.

"Whaddya say we call it a day here?" Josiah's lawyer asked, moving his phone away from his ear. He looked at the phone and stood up. "Let's talk in the hall real quick."

"Call it a day?" I lamented. Had we even started?

The three of us waded into the hallway and stood beside the officer, who yawned at our exit. Josiah's attorney chuckled through an apology that his client couldn't offer more, but insisted he could get him to open up.

"How do you plan to do that? He doesn't even know who Cee is, according to you," I retorted.

Both paused long enough to smirk. Josiah's attorney looked at Holden, and they exchanged a glance whose purpose seemed to be to confirm my naivete.

"I'll explain. She's new," Holden offered. It seemed to satisfy the attorney, and he nodded with the realization. They scrolled through the calendars on their phones for the next available date on which to meet, which would be a few weeks from now. There was no rush. The trial wasn't for a few months anyway.

"He's not going anywhere!" they agreed aloud, chuckling at the overlap. One offered, "Great minds . . ." as the other tapped his temple in lieu of finishing the old saying. My stomach turned at the hallway fellowship. My calendar was obviously irrelevant, as I would not be joining the next meeting.

I glanced back through the cracked door. Josiah's head was on the table, his knee-knocking resumed. The sound of metal clinking became more pronounced in the empty room.

Holden started toward the elevator. "Come on! You gotta keep up, Coates!"

I followed him a few steps before stopping. "Aren't you going to wrap up? Say goodbye?"

He guffawed: "Say goodbye? I didn't even say hello! You're the one shaking hands with them." The word "them" and the way he used it caught me off guard. It rolled around in my mind, as if a human had just described the absurdity of mingling with a savage brute.

I walked back toward the door to find the officer preparing Josiah for transport. His lawyer's phone found its way back to his ear, but he smiled at me with a slight head nod.

"May I?" I asked his attorney. He waved me over to Josiah.

"Take care of yourself, Josiah. Make sure your attorney is keeping you informed, okay?"

He didn't respond. He just stared at me with a questioning expression I couldn't quite place at the moment. I chose to believe it was because he didn't hear me.

I caught up to Holden, who was checking his phone under a hallway light. He looked up as I approached. I didn't break stride. He laughed. "Finally. You're in a hurry. Where was that energy before? Told ya you'd have fun. Better than sitting in your office, right?" he said as we retraced our steps through the cement asylum, forcing me to question whether I was the patient or the psychiatrist.

I stopped walking and turned to face him as I unleashed my anger. I questioned why that was supposed to be fun. Not only did I fail to see the humor in seeing a chained human in a basement, but his so-called informant wasn't informed. It looked to me to have been an avoidable waste of time.

"Not a total waste of time, Coates." The look of mischief returned as a smile stretched across his face. "He rode on the snitch bus over here. The other inmates will know that he didn't go straight to the courthouse for a hearing like they did. You don't wanna be a snitch in holding, trust me. I guarantee he'll suddenly remember something to avoid riding on that bus back tonight."

He pushed the elevator button to signal that his explanation had ended.

"Did you know that wasn't his brother?" I asked, my body still turned toward him as I watched the elevator numbers ascend from the basement.

"Huh?"

"Cee. Did you really not know that wasn't his brother?"

"Cee? Who's that?" he said, boarding the elevator. "Never heard of him." He winked as he pressed the button to my floor.

"He's going to get hurt. And for what? He doesn't even understand what he was supposed to know! He didn't know anything, but they're not going to believe that. Why would you do that? And why bring me along?"

"Crazy, right?" he said, intentionally misinterpreting my tone as collegial and congratulatory, as he searched for an affirmation that would not come. I stood staring at him for the duration of the ride. He looked up, watching the floor numbers pass, avoiding my glare. In an attempt at chivalry, he held out his hand, lightly pressing against the elevator door as it opened: "Ladies first."

I walked off the elevator, grappling with my emotions. We were silent as we moved through the halls. He stopped at the first open door, eager to hold court with a willing audience. The office was empty. By the third empty office, his disappointment morphed into curiosity.

"Where is everybody? Was there a happy hour?" He checked his phone to see if he had missed something.

With my office in sight, I cut off the prospect of a postgame wrap-up. "I have work to do, Holden."

He paused briefly in front of my office door, which we had left not even thirty minutes earlier. He tipped the file back with one hand and tapped it against my arm as he continued down the hall, spinning back as he strode away.

"I'll let you know if everyone's getting drinks later. Oh, and hey," he said, pointing at the dried blood on my finger, "remember you've still got blood on your hand."

He was right.

The blood was an immediate reminder of a complicity I did not intend. And yet there I was, brooding in the realization that I had blindly followed someone with the promise of fun, lured like a child with candy. But I was a woman who knew better than to take candy from a stranger, trading boredom for a saccharin high without regard for the consequences. Without regard for the inevitable low.

As I sat in my office, door closed, barricading myself inside for a momentary reprieve from accountability, I turned toward the window overlooking the garage ramp on the street below. I stared as an unmarked van ascended the ramp, briefly jerking back as it paused for the security claws to retract into the pavement. The windows were tinted, but its membership in the government fleet was apparent. I wondered if Josiah was inside that van as it drove away. Either it was heading to the courthouse to retrieve defendants who would realize that Josiah didn't board with them, or he would be perp-walked back into the jail as the sole passenger. Either way, he was marked.

I stood, pressing my head against the glass, straining to see what I knew would be obstructed from view. I wondered if he could see me too. I backed away from the window as the van turned in my direction. The sun was setting, the light in my office converting the windowpane into a mirror. I stood staring at my own reflection. The seal of the United States Department of Justice hung beside me on the wall. My eyes fixed on my own face. It now held the same questioning expression I had been unable to decipher on Josiah's as he sat watching me. I said aloud, "Who do you think you are?"

3

"I Want No Part of This"

*On the Older Black Woman Victim Who Pleads
for Lenience for a Young Black Defendant*

"My God, I want no part of this," she declared, exasperated. "You hear me, no part!" Her tone was kind but unyielding.

"Ma'am, I think you might misunderstand me," I began. "I'm not from the Police Department. I'm the prosecutor handling this case. As I'm sure you've seen from my letter, the defendant is pleading guilty in your case. We didn't get a response to our letter requesting you to give a statement. Did you receive the letter?"

"I did," she said, drawing out the last word into three syllables.

I knew the judge would ask for more of an assurance that we'd made every effort to solicit her opinion on a proposed sentence than the simple mailing of a letter. I'd just watched this judge berate my colleague over the same issue earlier that day, and admonish the other prosecutors in the room that they, too, were on notice. So I continued. "I was just following up to make sure you got it and inquiring as to whether you would like to provide what's called a 'victim impact statement' to the judge. You see, it's a way for the judge to take into consideration what you think would be an appropriate punishment for his crime."

"I'm aware of what a victim impact statement is." She was eager to end this call.

I persisted, intent on checking this off my own list. "It's your absolute right to provide one . . . or not. And I'm guessing from your statement, perhaps not, but I don't want to make any assumptions here. Would you like to provide me with that statement? You could do it in writing, or in court if you'd prefer."

"I didn't misunderstand you," she said gently. I could tell that she was smiling. "But let me be clear. I want no part of this."

In a confirmatory tone, I summarized her response. "Okay, ma'am, that is your right not to give a victim impact statement. I will annotate the file and alert the court that you have declined. I will also provide you with a letter with the hearing information in case you change your mind and would like to appear. Thank you for your—"

"Wait," she interjected. "How old was that boy?"

I thumbed through the police report. "Ah . . . twenty. He's twenty years old."

"Oh my Lord . . . when is this hearing?"

"Tomorrow," I confirmed, adding the specifics.

"I'll be there. I will be in that courtroom, do you hear me? Mark my words, I will be there!" She hung up the phone after a brief but courteous goodbye.

I stared at the receiver for a moment, wondering what it was about his age that had suddenly galvanized her. Neither her intonation nor her incredulity offered any hints.

I considered calling her back for a moment to get a preview, but something about her tone left me intrigued, and I decided to wait for her appearance in court. I annotated the file, filling in the details of our conversation, and distributed the remaining files on my docket among the prosecutors who were assigned to cover the corresponding courtrooms the next day. They would carry the files to the courtroom in the morning, and had left their rolling briefcases open outside the doors of their offices for that purpose. I stopped in my colleague Dan's office to hand him the two files I wanted him to carry for me the next day.

"I intend to be there tomorrow for this sentencing," I said, holding up the files. He leaned in to see the name and highlighted a line with his marker. I moved the files closer to keep him from having to squint. "I'm just gonna put these here in your briefcase with the rest of the files you're bringing over, since I gotta come straight from day care drop-off to the courthouse, alright? I'm probably not gonna have time to make a pit stop back at the office before I have to be in court."

"No problem," he said. "Been there myself. Is he crying when you drop him off yet? Drop-off went from a handoff to a twenty-minute ordeal."

"I've got it down to ten minutes now. Believe me—that's an improvement," I said, relating to his story. Only it wasn't my son who was the one crying. It was me, feeling guilty about having to drop him off with the sun barely up.

My day care required me to use masking tape to label each bottle with my son's name and the date the milk was extracted. My husband made fun of me for drawing hearts on the labels our son couldn't yet read.

"Well, he can understand shapes!" I'd retort, struggling to draw hearts and stars along a curved bottle.

"Why don't you draw the shapes while the tape's still on the roll? Before you rip the tape?" he'd say as he put the baby into his carrier and loaded him into the car.

We had this discussion every day, and I would repeat my same irrational rationale, refusing to be wrong. "Because obviously the tape roll is more curved than the bottle. Obviously," I'd repeat, anticipating his next statement.

"So maybe we just dispense with the shapes and just focus on the numbers and letters in the morning?" He'd playfully hold up the baby carrier to try to prevent me from throwing a wad of tape that would inevitably stick to my fingers anyway.

Our son required at least five full bottles during my workday now, and I was drinking water incessantly to keep up my milk supply. I would need to start supplementing with formula soon. My trial schedule wouldn't allow me the breaks I needed to pump as frequently as I needed to anymore.

My colleague brought me back to the moment as I turned to walk away.

"You able to keep up?" he asked.

"Excuse me?" My expression was cold.

"The water bottle. My wife always had hers once our nanny started," he said, pointing at mine.

"Oh . . . well, no nanny for me, but yes, I'm keeping up for now. Alright, I'm heading out. See you later. Thanks!" I tapped my water bottle on his doorframe as I left. Returning to my office, I looked out the window to the street below and saw my husband in the car, waiting. I waved in case he was looking up and gathered my belongings. I bounced out of the elevator and said good night to the guard at the door. When I got to our car, I pulled the door handle, only to find it locked. I waited for the click of the lock unlatching and tried again. I popped into the car with my purse on my lap and started to fill the air with a reenactment of my day as I waited for us to move.

"You forgetting something?" my husband asked. The car was still in park.

"Oh." I leaned it to kiss him.

He took the kiss and smiled through his response: "I meant the milk. I don't see the bag you usually carry."

I sighed, heaving myself back out of the car. My office neighbor smiled as I walked past her door with my thermos bag in hand. "Got milk?" she quipped, tickled by her own joke.

"Just you wait . . . ," I said, shutting off her lights to mess with her.

"I was leaving anyway," she said, laughing.

The next morning, I kissed my husband as he dropped me at the back entrance of the courthouse, where the security line was shorter. I didn't have much time to spare.

I headed into the courtroom where my cases would be heard by the assigned judge, hoping mine were not the first called. I needed a moment to catch my breath. I arrived in time to steal a seat along the wall, taking a moment to acclimate myself to today's audience before the judge entered the courtroom.

The moments spent waiting for any judge's entrance are always oddly the same. There's a flurry of anxious defendants and lawyers incessantly checking their phones and watches. Parents are straightening sons' ties, children are hushed, noses are blown, someone is speaking on their phone to give updates before being told they can't use their phone inside. The marshals walk to the clerk, who's got a story to tell and a list of defendants for the marshals to confirm are in the holding cell behind the courtroom. Double doors open and close, allowing the sounds of the hallway to drift in and alert you to the microcosm that is this particular courtroom. Defense counsel approaches the prosecutor to put a face to a name or solidify the deal, as defendants and interested members of the public lean over the railing that separates the spectator gallery from the well of the courtroom to get a prosecutor's attention to inquire when their case is going to be called.

I settled into the front row of the benches that are reserved, by unspoken rule, for counsel, and watched as a different colleague than the one I'd spoken to the night before was now assigned to handle the court's docket. She removed several dozen files from her rolling briefcase and nervously placed the files in lines on the table, alphabetically so that she could readily locate each when the courtroom clerk called a particular matter. I strode over to ensure that my two files were among them. Finding them, I returned to my seat, but not before letting her know that I was here to handle both. I tapped on one. "Don't let them call this case unless I'm here. I need to personally handle it."

"Oh, thank God. I have so many matters up today. I just switched with Dan. He was stuck in traffic and I was the dummy who answered the phone. So here I am!"

"Been there!" I said, remembering my conversation with Dan the night before while dropping off my files with him.

"So you're handling both of your sentencings, right?" she confirmed.

"Yes," I said as I grabbed the more difficult one and walked it back to my seat, which was now taken. I found a new one and settled in again. I watched my colleague order and then reorder the files, stacking them in cascading columns before switching to a big vertical stack before rearranging them into a horizontal spread. I wondered if I'd ever looked that nervous.

A gloved older Black woman wrapped in a charcoal wool coat and fur scarf approached the railing, briefly elevating her voice toward my colleague's back: "Excuse me, Ms. Coates?" she inquired. "Prosecutor Coates, I mean."

I couldn't immediately place her voice, and I paused to see what my colleague would say before I made a move to identify myself.

"Laura?" she asked, this time more familiar. "I told you I'd come today."

My colleague looked back, searching for me. I met her eyes and she motioned toward me as I stood to greet the woman. "I'm Laura Coates. How can I help you?"

She identified herself as the owner of the vehicle that had been stolen in my case. This was the file I had left on the desk, the easier of the two sentencings.

"Ah, yes," I said, immediately recalling how intrigued I'd been. "You decided to come. I'm glad you did."

"Yes, when you told me he was twenty, Laura, I just—can I call you Laura? I don't mean to be so presumptuous."

She laughed like a woman accustomed to holding court. She resembled an aged jazz singer, still physically in her prime. Her hair was perfectly coiffed in a silver bob. Subtle freckles adorned her face, and she spoke through plum lips accentuated by a peaked Cupid's bow.

"Laura's fine," I said, chuckling, eager for her to tell me what she intended to say and not to derail the conversation with formalities. "You were saying?"

"When you told me that he was twenty, I just thought to myself—"

A loud voice silenced the crowd, cutting her off. Irritated by the cliffhanger, I motioned for her to meet me in the hallway so that we could talk.

"No, it's okay," she said. "I only want to do this once today."

Reluctantly, I reclaimed my seat. Like clockwork, a marshal came to life in the moments before the judge's entrance, suddenly aware of the unnerving decibel level of the noise, and commanded everyone to be quiet. When the room fell silent, the marshal gave a second robotic command to rise, and with that a robed judge flew into the courtroom, eager to begin his docket. This particular judge's adherence to his schedule bordered on neurotic. He arrived

43

precisely two minutes before his cases were to be called, at 9:28. He sat down with gusto and spread his robe out on the side while adjusting his tie. The judge cleared his throat while he methodically placed his files, pens, and monitor just so. His Honor never looked up during this ceremonial display but seemed to revel in the notion that all eyes were fixed on him. At precisely 9:30 he would pinch his nose, inhale, place his hands on each arm of his chair, lean forward, eyebrows raised, and instruct the clerk sitting to his right to call the first case. Only when the defendant was standing behind the table would he look up. He would cock his head, briefly sizing up the defendant before turning to the prosecutor with a simple "Government?"

I watched as my colleague painstakingly made her way through the docket, delving into even the most benign details of the history of the case to bring the judge up to date on the circumstances that led to this case being on his docket on this day. I waited as the judge, meticulous in his approach, belabored each detail of the conditions of release. He could never be accused of making a hasty decision or leaving a stone unturned. This judge merely wanted to start on time, never end on time. As she placed each completed file into the case behind her, the prosecutor would steal a momentary glance at me, raising her eyebrows in what we both understood to be a lament about being in this courtroom, in front of this painfully slow-moving judge.

On any other day, my case would have been called after the dozens of misdemeanors were completed, and I would have had time to speak with the victim in the hall about her expected impact statement. But today the defense counsel was missing on a number of cases, and the judge turned to the matters where defense attorneys had checked in with the clerk to show that they were present and accounted for. The defense attorney in my case was one such attorney, and our case was promptly called. I would hear the victim's impact statement when the court did.

I rose from the bench and approached the swinging half door that separates the public gallery from the inner vestibule of the court, buttoning my jacket as I walked. I turned and motioned to the victim, imploring her to be patient. I smoothed the front of my skirt and folded my hands together, resting them on my thighs. As the defendant was brought from the holding cell, I indulged the judge's meticulous methodology, waiting for his invitation to state my name for the record.

"Laura Coates, on behalf of the United States, Your Honor," I said, as the defendant settled into place. He was handcuffed, in an orange jumpsuit.

"Oh my God, is that him?" the victim asked from the gallery.

The judge's eyes narrowed as he motioned to the marshal with indignation that someone had dared to disturb the silence. He banged the gavel once and admonished against any outbursts, no matter how subtle.

I apologized on behalf of the victim and alerted the court to her presence. The judge nodded, seemingly less offended by a courtroom novice who, but for the defendant's actions, would not be here.

After the admonishment, the judge nodded for me to give my allocution, a statement of facts I would assure the court I could have undoubtedly proven beyond a reasonable doubt in front of a jury. I had already provided these at the time the defendant entered his guilty plea, but the court wanted it on the record again as a precursor to the sentence that the judge was prepared to hand down today.

Just as at the time of his guilty plea, the defendant's attorney did not contest the facts or the government's ability to prove them. He also didn't contest the possible range within which he could be sentenced according to the guidelines, nor my sentencing recommendation. The only surprise left would be what the victim would say.

"Has the government made any attempt to secure a victim impact statement? In addition to the mailing of a letter outlining the victim's ability to do so?"

"Yes, Your Honor." This judge preferred responses in bite-sized pieces to give the impression that he was driving the conversation.

"And what attempts did you make to secure such a statement?"

"Your Honor, I sent a letter to the victim's last known address. She was contacted there by the officers at the time she was notified of the crime. I did not receive a response and followed up via telephone. I reached her yesterday afternoon, Your Honor."

"And did you inform her of her right to make a victim impact statement?"

"I did, Your Honor."

"And did she share her intent to provide such a statement?"

My eyes were beginning to glaze over. "Yes, Your Honor. She stated that she would provide one."

"And did she provide a written statement or is she present in court to deliver it verbally?"

"She will provide an in-court statement, Your Honor."

"Is she present in the courtroom at this time?"

"Yes, Your Honor. May I call her?"

"You may, yes."

I motioned for her to approach the lectern standing between the counsel tables.

"Your Honor, I have not consulted with the victim regarding her statement ahead of time," I felt compelled to add, unsure of what her position would be.

She strode toward the lectern, pausing briefly to look at the defendant. He lowered his eyes and searched the floor. Judging by how sheepishly he looked at her, I wondered if they knew each other.

The judge waited until she had reached the lectern before he spoke. "Now you will have the opportunity to speak. I know that you were eager to do so earlier," he said, recalling her outburst. He recited the speech he gave regularly on the purpose of this type of statement. Despite the fact that crimes committed within our communities affect us all, he said, it was important to hear from the person most deeply or directly affected. I listened intently, reciting along with him in my head. I'd heard it so many times.

He paused, alerting her to the fact that it was her opportunity to speak.

"Judge . . . Your Honor . . . ," she said, correcting herself gracefully. "May I?"

"Please," he said, leaning in to hear what was already being amplified by the microphone.

"I don't know *this* young man, Your Honor," she began. "But I know young men like him."

I stepped toward her, prepared to address any attempt to use this opportunity to put forth whatever stereotype she seemed to be referencing. Prepared for my assumptions, she held up her hand in protest, beseeching me to let her finish.

The judge leaned in farther, angling his left ear forward. I held my breath and wondered if the defense counsel would attempt a futile objection, if only to disrupt her train of thought. He seemed as intrigued as I was and stared intently.

"I know young men like him. My son was twenty once. And so were his friends. And so are other mothers' children. They were twenty once too, or at least you hope they will be. And likely as dumb as this young *boy* seemed to act that night. Understand I'm

47

not calling him . . . I'm not calling you . . . *dumb*." She had turned her body toward the defendant now. "But dumb-acting is what you'd have to be to steal a car, knowing there are cameras everywhere. In broad daylight. Dumb-acting is what you'd have to be acting like to flee the cops and lead 'em on some kind of high-speed chase. Dumb-acting is what you'd have to be to smash that car and run away, and try to pretend that it wasn't you when they stopped you. I heard everything that the prosecutor had to say. And it was my car. That *was my* car you crashed. But you know what?"

She paused for effect.

"I can afford my car. I can afford the insurance on that car. I'm seventy-three years old and I'm retired, and I didn't have anywhere to be the day I discovered it missing. I wasn't late to any appointment. I didn't have children to get back from school. I didn't have to run my husband to dialysis that day . . . he passed last September, you see."

This time she directed her comments to me. "When the police called me to tell me what had happened, I just called my son to come pick me up and bring me over to the station. My son, the one that used to act dumb just like you, came over and picked me up. And then I used my other car until I was able to settle the issue with my insurance company. There was no real harm to me. None at all. No one was hurt. I mean, the car was hurt, and the damage was bad, but no one is really even raising my insurance to an amount I can't afford. It didn't cost me anything to get it fixed." She was matter-of-fact.

"Now, if anyone should be upset, it should be me. That was my husband's car. And it smelled like him. It doesn't anymore. It smells like something else now. Maybe a little like him, but not like it did before this. And my husband and I used to really worry about our sons—all of them. We knew they'd make mistakes, and they did. But they had the chance to make 'em, and someone had the grace to let 'em fix those mistakes. I intend to be that person here." She turned toward me, smoothing the layers in the back of her hair.

"Like I told the prosecutor, Laura, yesterday. I wanted no part of this case. This prosecution. I didn't intend to be here, but then, Laura, when you told me he was twenty, I remembered the dumb mistakes my own children made. And I said to myself, this is a child. And a Black child in this country at that."

She turned back to the defendant. "I refuse to help anybody ruin his life over something I'm hardly studying. Not if the cause is some damage done to me that I didn't even experience. I read this letter that you sent, Laura. And, Your Honor, you made it clear today too. It says you wanted me to give a statement about the way that this crime has impacted my life. Well, it didn't really. Not at all. If anything, it was a minor inconvenience. Your Honor, don't make an example out of him for my sake. He's a child. He made a mistake. White children get to joy-ride. But this Black boy's chained on the other side of a table and you're asking me to help keep him that way." The judge removed his glasses, holding them in one hand, leaning his bottom lip on his knuckle. The courtroom was silent.

"I know what this so-called justice system does when it gets its claws into Black boys." The way she pronounced the word "boys" made it buoy in the air. "I want no part of that. I don't know if he has a record of some kind. I don't know how he's acted since he's been here. But I'm not about to let some boy pay for being dumb for the rest of his life when no one was hurt and the owner of that car he took doesn't even care about it. I want no part of it. Can I speak directly to this child, Your Honor?"

The judge nodded, seemingly transfixed.

"Look, you made a mistake. And it was a dumb mistake. People could've gotten hurt. You could have died trying to get away from being so dumb. But apparently God wasn't done with you yet. And

49

God isn't done with me yet. And today, I think you ought to get a second chance. There's normally a fine with this kind of thing, right, Your Honor?"

"Yes, ma'am," the judge said, surprisingly submissive to this woman who had no intention of yielding until she had finished making her point.

"Well, then, he should have to pay that fine to me. And I'll hold on to the money and even put it into an account for you and give it back when you're done being dumb. That's what I would do for my own children, and I'll do that for him."

She began placing her gloves back onto her hands, one by one, pressing down the gloves into the webs between her fingers, her eyes focused on their fit as she concluded. "I'm ready to leave this courthouse now unless you have any questions for me, Your Honor. I assume you'll do what you're going to do despite what I have said today. But in good conscience, I needed to say it. Can I go now, Laura?"

Entranced by her soliloquy, I had to remember that my role was more than that of an audience member waiting to applaud her rebuke of the victim impact statement as perfunctory but also the injustice within the system.

"Your Honor, may I excuse the witness?"

"Ma'am, thank you for your statement today . . . ," the judge responded.

She nodded as she walked back through the swinging doors and reclaimed her seat. Defense counsel elbowed his client and whispered something in his ear.

"Thank you, ma'am," the defendant called out, doing a double take as he glanced at the judge, unsure if he was supposed to say anything at all. He shut his eyes and tried to swallow any hope that her words had influenced the judge as he felt the judge's stare piercing into him.

She nodded at his quivering voice.

"What do you recommend, government?" the judge asked.

Moments ago, we had already recommended that he serve limited jail time, followed by a probationary period. The judge's very question seemed to invite my reconsideration in light of the victim's statement.

"Your Honor, the government's recommendation is consistent with analogous cases, the guidelines, and the statements of his pretrial officer. But the victim's statement is quite compelling and you are free to consider it in light of this now being described by her as a victimless nonviolent crime."

"Were officers made aware of her desire not to prosecute this case?"

The judge knew it didn't matter, but he was searching for a reason not to discount her wishes or signal to defendants that victim impact statements could negate a guilty plea.

"Remind me of the charges again, Ms. Coates . . ." His statement was delivered like a rhetorical question.

"Your Honor, he was charged with multiple crimes in addition to the underlying felony. As you know, the car owner's decision to report or prosecute would have no influence on the officers' decision to charge for his actions related to chase and the conduct thereafter. Her earlier statements, however, might have influenced the officers' decisions in this case had she perhaps been provided with information about the defendant sooner."

"And the guidelines . . ." Uncharacteristically, he was looking for an exit ramp.

"Your Honor, as you're aware, the sentencing guidelines indicate that probation is possible, with the option of incarceration in the event that the terms of his probation are not met. This would be consistent with how the court has handled other matters and

51

continues to be in line with the government's recommendations. But perhaps we can hear from the defendant in light of the impact statement?" Now it was my turn to lead the judge.

The defendant's youthful professions of remorse paled in comparison to his victim's aged eloquence. He was overwhelmed and unprepared, and the judge was hardly impressed. His counsel's eloquence, however, surpassed the victim's as he now tried valiantly to move the needle toward lenience.

"Government?" The judge asked a final time. I'd never seen the judge ping-pong his deference from one party to the other, and I had never seen him so sincerely interested in our recommendations. Still, I was reluctant to expend all of my ammunition on this case.

I knew there would be cases for which I'd have to use my credibility. Cases where lenience would be warranted regardless of a victim's statement in support of or to the contrary. I knew that I might get but one bite of the apple from this judge, and there were two files in my hand today. In the next case, there would be no surprise advocate, no eloquent defense counsel to champion his cause. That case would require the full attention of the court, and I would need to persuade the court why a departure from the guidelines was, in fact, justified. I couldn't risk compromising my perceived objectivity in this case, calling for the lenience I imagined was already a foregone conclusion. I wanted to be sure that when I did ask for lenience toward a defendant, the court would assign what was due.

This defendant had led officers on a high-speed chase, injuring one, and then fleeing with a significant amount of drugs in his possession. Asking for lenience here would have made the judge question my judgment in other cases.

"Your Honor, my recommendation stands." Frankly, it was already lenient enough.

The courtroom was silent. I could practically hear my own eyes blinking as I waited for the judge to speak. The victim was visible in my periphery, but I declined to meet her gaze.

The defendant's sniffle broke the silence. I looked over to see tears streaming down his face, his jawbone discernibly clenching along his ear. He looked every bit the man who now had the words that had escaped him at the critical moment. The very man who somehow knew that he'd missed his chance.

And yet the judge offered him that chance, giving him probation. As he was led into the holding cell to finalize his release, he looked back at the victim. She looked at me, disgusted. I knew she thought I was heartless, disappointed by my decision not to change my recommendation after hearing her statement. But I couldn't let her opinion affect me. I had to move on to my next case, and I knew that defendant would need an advocate.

When the clerk called the next case, the file was already in my hand. I waited for the defendant's attorney to make his way to the table. His defense counsel had to be nudged awake after the case was called a second time. As he walked through the swinging door, you could see that his client's file was practically empty. The marshals escorted his shackled client to the defense counsel's table.

When it was time for the defendant's attorney to identify himself and announce his client's presence for the record, he mispronounced his name. The defendant had no family, no champion, no ability to pay for an attorney; and I had no confidence in the ability of the attorney who had been appointed to defend him to effectively advocate for his client. Today's sentencing would seal his fate, but there was no eloquent victim impact statement or zealous defense attorney coming to save him. There was only me today. So I spoke: "Laura Coates, on behalf of the United States of America." And this defendant.

4

She Needed Me to Believe Her

On the Domestic Violence Survivor Afraid to Be Judged

We were the same age, born on the very same day. We even resembled each other: the same complexion, same pronounced cheekbones, the same shape of our lips, with a bridgeless nose. Our smiles were both ready, only hers had a reticence I hoped my own did not convey. We were even wearing the same lipstick.

I didn't mention our shared birthday as I sat across from her explaining why I didn't have a notebook or pen in front of me. It was my standard preface to a conversation with a victim in one of my domestic violence prosecutions. I explained that I did not want her to feel uncomfortable, as if she were watching someone further document what was likely the worst experience of her life, as if I were a detached court reporter simply transcribing her words rather than understanding the emotion with which she relayed them. I wanted her to know that I was hearing her, that I was fully present in the moment, and that what she had to say was so important that it deserved my undivided attention.

Truthfully, that was only part of the rationale. I did care, and she—and others—did deserve my undivided attention. But there was also a trial strategy at play. If I took notes, I might have to prematurely produce them to opposing counsel, who would be able to disregard the grand jury transcript, and use each word against the victim at trial. A savvy defense attorney would focus on our notes rather than her statements made under oath, and I needed the focus to be on that testimony. If they were going to challenge her on her story, I wanted it told to the grand jury, not when her guard was down in a moment of trust between just the two of us. We still preview the nature of a victim's testimony before the victim meets with the grand jury, but we just didn't keep a written record of it. We want the transcripts to speak for themselves.

I also never took notes because it broke my concentration, and more important, my eye contact. As much as I was listening, I was studying. Studying her eye movements, her facial expressions, the way she moved her hands and shifted uncomfortably in her seat. I studied the clearing of her throat, the movement of her hair from her cheek, the subtle way she pursed her lips before swallowing each time she said his name. I studied how she held my gaze until she spoke about him, and the way she tried to hide her shaking hands by pressing her palms together as if in prayer and rigidly confining them between her thighs. I studied how quickly she responded to questions and to what extent she was comfortable with the lulls. I watched to see which direction her eyes looked—she always looked up as if searching the ceiling—when she answered questions about physical locations and their relative distance from one another.

I studied the way she was studying me, feeling her eyes scan me as I thumbed through the file, trying carefully, neurotically, to straighten the paperwork so as not to show even the corner of the police photographs that captured her facial injuries. They were jutting out; someone had carelessly punched holes into the top, off-center, and the photos were shamelessly trying to draw attention to themselves.

She already knew that the man who brutalized her just days before had been arrested. Given the police description of the case, I didn't need her to convince me that a crime had occurred. I just needed to explain to her the process of testifying before the grand jury and how this stage was not akin to a full trial. I explained that these jurors would help me to determine not whether to file charges but which to file, and that in front of the grand jury today she would tell what had happened to her, careful not to use the word "story." I didn't want to imply that I was being cute and didn't believe her, that her testimony was conjured or embellished. I used the word "truth" and implored her to speak hers. My appeal became a psychological motif, woven throughout our pre–grand jury discussion.

"The only thing I want you to do is tell the truth. If you can't remember something, it's okay, just tell the truth. Don't try to make something up because you think everyone expects you to know it. Just tell the truth. If you remember anything we've discussed today, it's that I want you to tell the truth. Even if you think it makes you or someone else look bad. Don't worry about that. Just tell the truth. It's not up to you whether someone chooses to believe your truth. But please tell the truth . . ."

The repetition was intentional overkill, belabored ad nauseam to create a memory. I had seen so many defense attorneys try to suggest to the jury that the prosecutor had helped the witness concoct a story: "What did the prosecutor tell you before your testimony to the grand jury? What did they *need* you to say?" The word "need" was particularly effective in getting a recanting witness who has had a change of heart to pretend that she was manipulated. Without the repetition, a witness was more likely to stumble when trying to remember my entreaty at the time of trial. I would also place our conversation on the record right after she swore an oath.

"Now, we spoke in my office a few moments ago. What is the one thing I asked you to do?"

"Tell the truth."

"During our conversation, I didn't take any notes or write anything down, did I?"

"No, you didn't."

"And did I tell you what to say here today?"

"You told me to tell my truth. Just tell the truth."

"No matter what?"

"Yes, just tell the truth."

I continued with my statements about truth until her head bobbed emphatically and her expression said to move on. I moved on to setting the scene of what to expect with the grand jury. I began describing the format of questioning and the room layout so she knew what she'd be walking into. With each statement, she nodded but swallowed laboriously. She asked what time she would do this.

"Now," I said, "as soon as you're ready. They'll be ready for us in a few moments. We just need to head down there."

"Is it at the courthouse?"

"No, the grand jury meets here in our office. They're only a few floors down. They have a special section just for them."

"So, you said they can ask me questions, too?"

"They can, but I'll stop them if they ask anything inappropriate. Don't worry. I'll protect you." As soon I said the word "protect," I wanted it back.

"Do I need protection in there? Are they going to, like . . ."

I interjected before she could find the right word. "I'm sorry. I just mean that I will make sure you're comfortable. The grand jurors are just regular people, and they may have a question about something you said that maybe they didn't hear, or ask about how to spell a name, or they may ask how you're feeling. It can be very difficult to hear about what you experienced, and they might just want to say something supportive or just make sure you're okay."

It was then that she began to cry. She was not okay.

As if I didn't know the reason, I asked, "What's wrong?" I offered a string of comforts based on my assumptions about the nature of her apprehension without waiting for a response. "Don't worry," I said. "He is not going to be there. Remember he's locked up. Your son is safe at school, and the jurors will really just be there to listen. They may ask a few questions, but I will be there with you. No one is there to hurt you or judge you, and you can take a break whenever you want. You only have to do this once, and then it can be over." She would only have to do this once if he took my plea offer and avoided trial.

I stood, hoping that my words had at least temporarily placated her enough for her to begin her testimony. There were only a few slots available to go before the grand jury today, and I didn't want to miss her window. I knew full well what can happen when victims have a day to ponder—their resolve wanes, their cooperation dissipates, and if given the choice, many would never return. Even if they did return, under the power of a subpoena, their truth would become a story that conveniently excluded an antagonist.

But I also knew that each time someone was murdered at the hands of a lover in our jurisdiction, our office scanned the domestic violence cases to see if any charges had been brought against the assailant and, if not, the reasons the case did not go forward. "She cried in my office and seemed like she didn't want to talk about it today" was not a box you could check to justify your reticence. Her testifying today could save her life, and I knew it. The fear that your decision not to prosecute a case would have fatal consequences was always in the back of our minds. My concern wasn't limited to her—I didn't know who else might be victimized by him. Abusers are emboldened when they are not held accountable. I had an obligation to prosecute him now to prevent harm to others in the future.

"Can we just . . .?"

I thought I knew what was coming. "Can we just what? Forget it happened?" I said, gently finishing her thought. I leapfrogged to impatience intentionally.

"No, that's not what I was going to say. I . . . just can't believe I'm here. That this is my life right now." She whimpered as she cried, cupping her mouth with her left hand and leaning on the elbow rest.

I pivoted toward the back table to grab a tissue box and swung back to her. I glanced at the clock on my desk phone. I always padded a witness's arrival time, so the grand jury was not yet waiting on us.

I held out the box and she reached over to take one. She was still wearing her engagement ring. My eyes lingered on it as I rested my chin on the back of my hands, pushing my bottom lip up in a way that formed a frown. I placed the box down on the desk in front of her, my mind recalling the photographs sitting in the file under my elbows. The blood streaming from her eyes, nose, and mouth. The faded marks along her body. The boot mark on her back from being stomped on. The hair ripped from the side of her head as she grabbed her son and ran to the door, managing to open the door and throw the little boy into the hallway of the apartment building for safety as she screamed for someone to help . . . him. The photos showed the severe bruising around her neck from the choking she had endured while she blocked the doorway to protect her son, not reaching for her own neck to pry the boy's father's hands off but instead grabbing the doorframe so her body would not yield, tearing her nails in the process. She had lost consciousness hearing her young son scream her name.

Witnesses told police that the boy's father—her fiancé—had spit on her before walking back into the apartment to sit on the couch. They had watched him through the open door, screaming at himself and punching the sides of his head with his own fists as he shouted for his son to come sit beside him. An older woman had intervened, shuttling the boy into her home with her grandson and locking the door while she called the police. Neighbors yelled from the hallway that they had already called the police as one resident knelt beside the victim, beseeching her to wake up.

By the time the police arrived, she had regained consciousness. Police found her fiancé holding her in his arms as he called her "baby" and wiped blood from her face. The witnesses quickly re-layed the facts as the police separated the two, safeguarding her as they tried to assess the full extent of her injuries. The police officers handcuffed the fiancé immediately, denying his request to remain on the scene until his mother could be notified to pick up the lit-tle boy. The neighbor who had taken the boy into her apartment invited the officers inside. She wanted to keep him there until she could reach his maternal grandmother. She didn't feel right about letting him go with his father's family. She questioned a family that could raise such a man—someone who could do something like that. Once the officers understood that the assault had occurred in front of the boy, they refused to let the defendant speak to the child, disgusted by his show of concern now. The officers asked the vic-tim permission to use her phone to contact her family to come see about the boy. An officer waited inside the neighbor's apartment, playing with the little boy until his maternal aunt arrived.

After her testimony before the grand jury today, I would have the responding officers testify to what had happened when they had arrived on the scene. Her memory would be limited to the assault prior to losing consciousness. She was still piecing it together from the neighbor's whispers and her son's nightmares. One officer was in the courthouse testifying in a trial today, and I made a mental note to text him to stand by for his testimony after she left.

She exhaled for a moment, wiping her eyes and staring at the tissue as she folded it over.

I began the next sentence with her name, saying, "What he did to you, you didn't deserve that. No one does. What he did to you was unimaginable. And it was in front of your son."

"His . . . *own* . . . son . . . ," she said aloud to herself, nodding and pausing after each word. "And all I was doing was trying to make a point about him taking care of our son when this happened! I didn't think . . . I didn't think . . ." She fought to catch her breath, choking on her sobs.

My heart felt heavy. While this was not the first time he had become physical, she couldn't have predicted how violent his response would be over a fight about feeding their son. Earlier that day, she had been out with the boy and had tried to buy him lunch at a fast food restaurant. Her card was declined and she didn't have any cash on her. An employee offered to give the lunch to her for free, but she was too embarrassed and left. She tried to call the bank to figure out why her account was overdrawn. She was sure she had just gotten paid, and rent had not even been taken out yet. She tried to call her fiancé, but he did not answer the phone. Had he been using her card again? She put the question to him in a text. No answer. More than two miles from home, she didn't want to have to walk in the extreme heat. She didn't have enough money on her Metro card, and without a working debit card, she couldn't refill the Metro card. She chose not to call her family to come pick them up since she knew they'd ask where her fiancé was and she didn't feel like fielding their judgment today.

On the way home, she had tried to entertain her hungry child, promising to make him his favorite lunch when they got back. She stopped at a small playground, hoping that she could bide her time until her fiancé answered the phone and came either to pick them up or bring them back to the restaurant. Help never came. By the time they reached their apartment building, she was drenched in sweat. She had carried her son for the last half mile because he was too tired to walk. She was dialing her fiancé's number again as she turned the key in her front door. She found her fiancé sitting on the couch inside an air-conditioned living room, playing a video game. His phone was on the coffee table vibrating in front of him.

"Why'd you keep calling me?" he asked without even looking in her direction. "You woke me up," he complained.

She stormed in and snatched the controller.

The photographs illustrated his reaction.

"I saw the police photographs and . . . "

"You saw the photos?" She seemed surprised.

"Yes, I saw them. I'm sorry this happened."

"Will they see them today?" she asked.

"Yes."

She looked uncomfortable and closed her eyes.

"Would you like to see them?" I asked, unsure if the memory would encourage or alienate her.

She nodded.

"Are you sure?" I asked.

"No."

I wanted the grand jury to see her reaction in real time and hesitated. I needed raw emotion to persuade the grand jury, and it would be impossible to replicate. "I only want you to have to see these once. If we need to show the grand jury, we will, okay? I don't want to upset you further. I'm sorry this is happening."

"What are you thinking?" she asked me pointedly.

"What am I thinking?" I repeated, feigning confusion to buy myself time—not to reflect but to decide whether my honest response would be cruel or helpful. I was staring at a woman who was still wearing her engagement ring, and I wondered if *she* was thinking about still marrying him. I was thinking that there was a chance that she might go back to her abuser and that he may have also been physically abusive to their son. I wondered what else the boy had seen. I was thinking that we were only here because she had been subpoenaed. I wondered, if the assault hadn't been carried out into the public hallway, whether we would have ever found ourselves face-to-face today. I was thinking about the emotional shame she felt, even though there was no intellectual justification for her blaming herself for what had been done to her. I was thinking that, if I were her, I'd use the prosecutor's answer to this very question as a justification to do what I wanted to do. If the answer felt judgmental, I'd retaliate by walking away. If the answer felt compassionate, I'd reward the prosecutor by being agreeable. I answered in a way that would motivate me.

"Yes, what do you think about all this?"

"I think it's absolutely horrible that someone who says they love you would treat you like this," I didn't elaborate, reluctant to risk infusing her impending testimony with my own personal opinion. I glanced meaningfully at the art on my wall—drawings made by my own preschool son. I wanted her to know, without my saying it, that she was speaking to another mother.

"You have kids?"

"Yes, a little boy."

"And what would you have done?"

"You mean, what could I have done differently? Nothing! It wasn't your fault."

"Do you think I'm stupid?" Her question was sincere, not attacking or rhetorical, and I felt sorry that she felt self-conscious.

"No. I don't think you're stupid." I tried to sound emphatic without being dismissive of the question. The truth was, one's circumstances weren't really a reflection of intellect; they were a reflection of choice, or lack thereof. Whether she would make the choice that was best for the trial remained to be seen. I wanted her to come to her own conclusion about what she needed to do for herself and her child. I knew that it would be better for her to feel powerful against her abuser by making the choice to testify today rather than having me remind her of the reality: under the subpoena, she would have no choice but to testify today.

"But you think I'm weak, don't you?"

"Why would I think you're weak?" I wanted her to realize she was projecting more than I was judging. She stared at me searchingly. I repeated my question. "Why would I think that you're weak? Why do you think that I feel that way about you?"

"Look, I know you're judging me. I saw the way you looked at my ring. Do you wanna know why it's still there?" I thought I had been more subtle in my reaction to seeing it.

"You don't need to explain anything to me." I'd been down this road before. I knew my statement wouldn't stop her from explaining, and, frankly, I wanted her to try.

"I can't get it off!" she screamed, her voice cracking at that octave. "My hand is swollen and I can't take it off. I tried! Look! Watch!"

She began trying to pry it off, but it was trapped below a swollen joint of a finger with a severed nail. She yanked away with both her arms bent at the elbows, parallel to the ground.

I hadn't expected that response, and my heart sank at the realization that I had judged, and now misjudged, her. I felt guilty

65

watching her struggle to disprove my assumption that her ring's placement on her hand was welcome. I wondered what other assumptions I had made.

"It's okay. I understand," I said. "Please don't hurt yourself." She was grimacing as she struggled.

"No!" she protested. "You don't understand! This is not my life. I'm not just some stupid woman who would let someone put their hands on them and take it."

I bristled at the word "stupid." That's not what I thought of her and was now concerned what my earlier facial expressions might have conveyed. I said her name again. "You're not stupid. And you didn't *let* this happen to you," I offered instead. I maintained eye contact to avoid being misunderstood.

"This has never happened before! We've fought but he's never done this to me!"

The police report said otherwise. "He's never put his hands on you before?" I sought clarification at the risk of sounding condescending. The grand jury would ask, and I had to be prepared.

"Never like this!" She furrowed her brow as her jaw bobbed, suspended. She chose her next words carefully. "So you are judging me." She nodded in affirmation without waiting for my response.

"No. I don't want you to misunderstand anything I've said, so let me be very clear with you. I'm not here to judge you, and I am not judging you. I believe you. If I didn't, well, frankly, you wouldn't be here right now. Look, you don't need to convince me of anything. You have your reasons to stay or go. It's none of my business what you decide to do with your life or your relationship. Legally, he can't come near you or contact you in any way. There's a temporary court order in place. If he violates it, he will be prosecuted for that, too. And I'll be the one to do that. But the order is not in place forever, and unless the grand jury indicts him, well, I can't keep him away even if I tried. Once it's gone, you'll do what you want."

"You think I'll go back to him?"

"I haven't thought about it." I lied. I had. And I assumed she might. Regardless of the injuries, I had seen initially cooperative victims become adversarial too many times to ignore the possibility. Even after the swelling in her hand had gone down, the ring could very well remain. And as a prosecutor, I had to prepare for every contingency, including the effect their potential reunification could have on my trial strategy. My judgment or advice wouldn't change her mind. It wouldn't even factor into the equation. It's one of the reasons a victim's desire to go forward is almost irrelevant. Federal prosecutors are not the personal attorneys of an individual victim. They advocate on behalf of the United States and all of the people who don't want to be victimized in the future. The government doesn't have the luxury of being emotionally fickle and still able to deter future conduct, even when it wants to do so.

A victim's preference for prosecution only comes into play when you are assessing the strength of witnesses. If no one else witnessed the attack, it could come down to he said, she said. If either is uncooperative, without independent corroboration, the case cannot proceed. Here, we had eyewitness accounts. Technically, I no longer needed her testimony to prove the case, but I wanted it, and I had a still cooperative victim mere feet from the grand jury, albeit one who seemed to need my approval.

I understood why—her need for approval wasn't specific to me. It seemed she was projecting her own fears and assumptions of what others might think of her based on her having judged others who had been in the very unfortunate position in which she now found herself. Now she was the target of her own prior assessment that a woman victimized by her abuser was stupid, and it was intolerable.

67

She needed me to believe that she was different, as she'd always assumed she was—the way everyone believes they are.

But this moment was beyond either of us. She wasn't alone in her denial, and she was certainly not the one who should have borne the blame. Our society denies the prevalence of domestic violence and actively seeks to discredit its victims. Perhaps it's a subconscious refusal to acknowledge that type of cruelty. Perhaps we fall victim to our own assumptions about the choices people make, or are left with.

Our collective approach exerts an emotional, psychological, and physical hold over victims that is nearly as powerful as the hold their abusers have over them, and it has a chilling effect. We somehow have lulled ourselves into believing that the issue is black-and-white: stay or go. We ignore the economic, familial, and psychological dynamic that creates, for so many, a barrier to leaving. We belittle people for their choices and pretend the choices themselves don't feel like illusions.

She needed me to see her the way she saw herself: as a strong, capable, resilient woman who could compartmentalize emotion with ease.

"We look like we could be sisters," she suddenly said.

"Yes, we do." Twins, I thought, making it all the more jarring to have seen the injuries in the photographs, and the swelling distorting her face today. The swelling reminded me of just how recent this attack was: it had happened two days ago. I suspected our hairstyles would have been the same had she not had to manipulate the bald patch rendered at the hands of her beloved. Perhaps similar earrings had her earlobe not been split by him.

She self-consciously touched her ear, seeming to read my mind.

"I'm smart, you know," she said, lifting her chin like a child telling a bully she didn't care what he thought.

"I know. Very smart. And very brave." She seemed reluctant to believe me, resigned to believe that she was just another victim and I was just patronizing her to manipulate her to do what I wanted. She felt raw, exposed, and vulnerable, and she was doubting herself. She was saying the right thing, doing the right thing, but her conviction had yet to catch up to her words. I recognized that feeling in myself and wanted desperately to reassure her.

"I mean it. You are." I was afraid my words were being misjudged. We had switched roles. Now it was I who wondered what she was thinking about me and whether she questioned that I meant what I said. It had become a survival tactic to emotionally distance myself from what I was hearing in these cases, allowing me to evaluate the merits of the case objectively. If I became too emotionally invested, I was afraid that it would not only compromise my professional judgment but add the already agonizing prospect of failing to convict. Now I wondered if the survival tactic itself had failed me.

My office phone rang, alerting me that the grand jurors were waiting for us. The clock was now ticking. "We'll be right down," I said, locking eyes with a scared woman circling defeat as I hung up the phone.

"It's time?" she said nervously.

"You asked what I was thinking. You want to know the truth?"

She raised her eyebrows expectantly.

"I've met a lot of women—men, too, of course—who have sat where you are right now. They've sat where you're sitting and told me they were strong. And they were. They've told me what they would never do, what they would never put up with, what they couldn't forgive, how much they hated the person, or what they were going to do to protect their children. And they meant every word. I know they did. The hard part for me to think about is what will happen after today—and I know, this wasn't done to me. I'm not the one who was hurt, and I wouldn't ever suggest that I know what it's like to be in your shoes. I'm not the one who has to make the choices that you are now being forced to make or face the circumstances that you will have to deal with—believe me. But I do carry you with me. I will fight for you as if it did happen to me and so it doesn't happen to anyone else, ever. The hard part for me is watching what comes next, what you will do tomorrow or the next day and the next day, through the trial, if there even is one. After the trial. I never want to make predictions, but trying to help keep you safe without having any control over the choices that you will make to help me do that—it's a difficult thing. Not everyone makes my job easy, you understand what I'm saying?"

She stared at me, silent.

"But there's something about you that makes me believe that tomorrow . . . I'm just hoping that this will be different."

She lifted her head. "I am different."

"Okay, then, prove it. But not to me. Not for me. Come on. It's time to go. Just remember to tell the truth. Tell the grand jury the truth. Tell yourself the truth."

I stood, walking to the hall with the file in hand before she could think. She grabbed her purse. Startled by the abruptness, she followed me down the hall.

As we walked, we passed a little boy who was nestled into the hall nook, playing with a wooden bead roller coaster. I knew that his presence in our office meant that he was likely the victim of violence or the child of someone who had been victimized and who had no choice but to bring him along. I paused to be sure he saw a friendly face.

"Having fun?" I said as we passed.

He pretended to be invisible, smiling as he covered his own eyes. He didn't understand the rules of the game, and she and I laughed.

"Where'd he go? Can you see him anymore?" she said. In that moment, we were just two mothers who understood the rules of the game instinctively.

"No! I can't see him either! I'm not sure we'll be able to find him—he must be a superhero!"

"I'm right here!" he said, removing his hands from his eyes.

We both feigned surprise as he laughed in his excitement to have pulled one over on us.

Our smiles remained as we waited for the elevator, grateful for that brief moment of levity. I wondered if we were his. We stepped inside, trading glances and closed-mouth smiles but then staring at the floor as the numbers flashed above.

The elevator stopped and I looked at her. Her eyes were closed and she exhaled audibly, briefly puffing her cheeks.

I led her to the grand jury and asked her to wait outside for just a moment while I introduced the case to the jurors. I only had an hour before the grand jury had to review a different case, and I would need every single minute of it. I came back out to the hallway and invited her into the room. She paused.

"Do I look alright?" she asked, straightening her back and smoothing her hair back toward her bun. Her hand lingered near the bald patch she tried to cover.

"Yes, you look like me," I said, winking.

I opened the door, letting her scan the room for a moment before walking inside.

"It's okay," I said. "I'm right here with you. Just one foot after the other, right?"

She nodded and stepped inside.

I introduced her by name to the expectant audience as the door closed behind us.

"Are you two related?" one of the retirees on the grand jury asked as she sat in the witness chair. We smiled.

A few weeks later, I was standing in front of the courtroom finalizing his guilty plea before the judge.

The judge asked if the victim wanted to make a statement before he sentenced the defendant. She had already indicated that she would not be there, but I turned to scan the courtroom to be sure. We had a written statement she had prepared with a victim advocate ready to be read aloud to the judge in light of her absence.

Instead, a voice called out. "I'm here, Your Honor!"

I was surprised to see her in the courtroom and wondered what her decision to speak in person meant. I stepped aside and held out my hand for her to have the floor as she made her way to the lectern. The defendant looked at her wistfully. The expression in their eyes matched. I looked back at the judge, reluctant to watch the scene unfold.

I held out the printout of her written statement for her, wondering if it was now obsolete. She made a point to take it with her left hand, displaying it to me awkwardly. The ring was gone, along with the swelling. But the indent it left from having just recently been removed was still visible.

I pretended not to notice the indent, because she needed me to believe her.

And I wanted to.

5

That's Not Me

On the Real Case of Mistaken Identity

I know what it is like to be mistaken for less than I am because of the way that I look. To be preemptively defined and judged by the most unflattering depictions, even when those depictions are clearly the figment of an ignorant imagination.

My race has always informed my objectivity and willingness to extend the benefit of the doubt. The presumption of a stereotype is that if a person does not conform to it, they are the exception. Racial stereotypes prevail even in the presence of incontrovertible truth. The lie consistently prevails, to the detriment of people of color. When you are a member of the race whose intolerable mistreatment was condemned only recently in your own mother's lifetime, you are guaranteed to be victimized by racism.

Blackness is an implicit charge in the criminal justice system. Black defendants must defend against the charge as much as the stereotype that negates a presumption of innocence. They may find their own name at the end of "The United States versus," but I assure you, their first line of defense will have to be combating the historic mistreatment, prejudice, and racist attitudes toward them—it is the Black defendant versus the history of the United States.

I understand both the myth of the stereotype and the reality of how it is wielded against people. The often insurmountable hurdle of trying to prove that you are not who they say you are. I have toiled under the weight of the inaccurate assumptions of inadequacy, ineptitude, and idiocy my entire life. And I'm perhaps regarded as one of the fortunate ones—fortunate to have suffered the adversity of assumptions but also to recognize and capitalize on the value of being so easily dismissed when who I am runs counter to your definition of who I should be.

Because of my own personal experience witnessing the pervasiveness of these stereotypes inside the Justice Department (let alone outside it), I could never be dismissive of an allegation that a Black person had been made to answer for the ignorance of another, let alone a Black defendant's claim of racial profiling or mistaken identity. It was indeed probable to me that the defendant could have been the victim of an assumption. And if the defendant raised the issue, I had to look into the matter before proceeding.

Yet my colleagues at the Department of Justice thought I was naive to indulge, even for a moment, claims of mistaken identity. It was like a form of cognitive dissonance. We frequently commiserated over certain police officers' judgment, tactics, and selective use of force. We would discuss the civil rights era and our shared interest in protecting the most vulnerable among us. Yet when there was any intersection of the two—mistaken identity and force—there appeared to be no acknowledgment that such claims were even plausible. Many of them dismissed wrongful arrest due to mistaken identity as an urban legend that no one could ever corroborate with specificity, an all-too-common excuse defendants gave. It was reduced to a hypothetical and summarily dismissed as paranoia.

There was always a tension brewing beneath the surface between those who were skeptical of the system and those who were skeptical of the people impacted most by it. At times it wasn't clear which camp you were in. Some days you were weary from having to fight against the system in the pursuit of justice. Other days you were wary of trusting those who were supposed to fight with you. You compartmentalize. You wonder whether your presence in the system perpetuates injustice or disrupts it.

After all, we were not investigators, not detectives. We did not make the arrests or give the Miranda warnings. We played the hand that we were given, and the hand was given by the cops' decision to arrest. The police controlled the deck. I vacillated between wondering if my skepticism was warranted or not, until one moment validated it completely.

Standing before a particularly persnickety judge, I was handling the government's matters on her calendar docket that day. No trials were scheduled, just status hearings and a few sentencings. The prosecutors assigned to the matters before the court had dropped off their files with a memo stapled to the front explaining how to handle them. The memos gave the background, the requested dates for motions to be filed, the pendency of plea discussions, and the timeline for discovery to be handed over.

Short of trial, it is customary for a prosecutor to handle matters not assigned to her. The court considered the government's attorneys fungible. As long as the stand-in could credibly articulate the government's position, it made no difference to the court who argued on behalf of it. Knowing this, prosecutors delegated the more mundane aspects of their most inconsequential cases to the prosecutor assigned to cover that courtroom, that judge, that day. On days I was assigned to cover a particular courtroom, one by one, I would handle the matters, annotate the file, and place it in my rolling briefcase, symbolically checking the matters off my list. I would place the files in my colleagues' mailboxes when I returned to the office with annotated notes to the file.

The clerk called the next item on the docket as I was putting away the file for the previous one, and I turned to locate the corresponding file on the desk. There was no memo, only a sentencing recommendation scribbled onto a line on the file itself. I waited for the court's prompting to present the government's position.

A Black defendant in his thirties approached the defense table with his attorney, also a Black man in his thirties. The attorney asked for the court's indulgence while he explained why this case should not go forward.

"Government?" the judge said, seeking my objection.

I was unfamiliar with the case and had no basis on which to protest.

"I'm not assigned to this matter, Your Honor, so I'd ask for his rationale before I can meaningfully respond."

She sighed dramatically. "Proceed."

The lawyer began by noting his frustration that the assigned prosecutor was not here to address this issue. The prosecutor had also failed to return his multiple calls and emails. He had been unresponsive to his letters or requests to resolve this issue in advance of this hearing date.

"I understand you're not the assigned prosecutor," the defense counsel said, turning toward me, "but I want his lack of responsiveness on the record. We should not be here today. My client should not be here today. His life has been turned upside down all because the Metropolitan Police Department can't tell two Black men apart!" He pointed with outstretched hand to the gallery as if the department itself was an individual seated in the courtroom.

He passionately claimed that the police had arrested the wrong man on a warrant for his failure to appear in court. Yes, his name was the same as the other man's. Yes, they were about the same age. Yes, he had been in the area of the warrant squad that day. A warrant was out for failure to appear at trial for the brutal assault against a woman with a child by the man of the same name.

Upon being picked up by the warrant squad, he was permitted to retain personal counsel, was temporarily released, and was required to appear before this judge. The shallow file was a procedural mess. The sequence of events that had led us to this hearing wasn't immediately clear. I regretted not having reviewed the file with the assigned prosecutor and knew I'd have to glean the full purpose of today's hearing from the judge's lead.

As the judge read the defendant the riot act for wasting the court's time, his counsel repeatedly interrupted to insist that he was not that person.

Each time, the judge dryly responded, "Yes, I understand. You're not that person anymore."

"No! I'm not that person, period!" he protested. The judge promptly admonished him to communicate only through his attorney.

His attorney continued in vain, pleading his case to the disinterested judge. Finally the attorney turned toward me: "Madam Prosecutor, help me out here."

I was intrigued by his insistence, but annoyed by his lack of specificity and proof. This wasn't the first time I'd heard a defendant profess his innocence—it was the precursor to every trial—but it was rare to hear someone claim mistaken identity at this stage in the game, and I assumed there'd be more than a bald assertion that "it wasn't me."

Before I could respond, the judge laughed aloud—not just a laugh, a guffaw—and said, "Well, she's not going to help you," as she nodded toward the marshals to handcuff the defendant. She proposed to hold him in jail until a new court date could be set.

His attorney held up his hands in defeat and said, "Look, I tried. That's all we can do."

I watched as the defendant's eyes flickered across his attorney's face, searching for some semblance of persistence. Finding none, he advocated for himself, again asserting his innocence: the warrant squad hadn't done their job correctly.

Again the judge laughed, and then, taking offense at the insinuation of sloppy work by the warrant squad, she rolled her eyes with impatience. She swiveled her chair toward me, smirking as if to say, "Likely story." She leaned forward, crossing her arms, and volleyed her head emphatically from me to the defendant. "So you're telling me that the warrant squad and the police officers and the mug shots and, my word, the whole world has conspired against you? We all got it wrong?"

She turned to me, fully expecting camaraderie, and robotically said, "Government, what do you want to do?" As she asked the question, the marshals were already handcuffing the defendant. I looked up, admittedly doubtful that the man was telling the truth, but, frankly, something about watching a White woman laughing at and belittling a Black man from her perch based on the misguided assumption that police were infallible profoundly annoyed me. I resented her incredulity and obnoxious tone so much that I was compelled to pause.

"Your Honor, I don't see the humor in this. There's a more respectful way to address this issue, wouldn't you agree?" I posited, and asked to address the man directly.

Taken aback by my refusal to join her laughter and my willingness to shame her, the judge indulged me, though she barely hid her irritation that I was prolonging this spectacle. As if I were a dog, she warned me that I was on a short leash.

I turned, beginning with the questions the judge should have led with instead of laughter, and asked the defendant why he hadn't raised this issue before. With pleading eyes, he told me that he had, but that no one would listen to him. He claimed that the officers just kept saying that they didn't believe him, and laughed at him repeatedly. The victim had never appeared for any hearing, and due to victim security and privacy laws, he didn't have any way to contact her. His lawyer and an investigator had attempted to find her, but her whereabouts weren't known. And, according to the police, she wasn't cooperative anyway. He said that he could prove he wasn't the man we were looking for if someone would just give him a chance to explain. The judge interrupted him. I interjected.

"Your Honor," I began, feigning deference toward a woman I now didn't respect, "there's no harm in looking into it. If he's lying, we can easily bring him into custody. The marshals are right there. If he's telling the truth, the warrant squad needs to know so they can find the right person." I was becoming increasingly annoyed at her unnecessary obstinance. "Can we have a brief recess?"

The judge threw down her pen. "Fine, if you want to waste your own time, then go compare his fingerprints. In the meantime, get one of your colleagues to stand in for you." She knew full well I was already the person assigned to stand in for other prosecutors that day. "Be quick about it. I don't have time for this."

Time, I thought. If convicted, the government would be prepared to ask for this man to serve more than a year in prison. The outlandishness of her demand refocused me. "You want me to compare his fingerprints to what, exactly, Your Honor? I'm not a fingerprint expert. You want me to hold 'em up to the sunlight?" I knew that my directness could very well infuriate her. But she was a former prosecutor and knew just how absurd her request was. She had a habit of berating attorneys and seemed to enjoy the public humiliation inflicted. Time and again I watched her exploit a prosecutor's deference, berating them with impunity. They feared retaliation down the line and often made the choice to submit. But I had been before this judge so many times, successfully navigating her unjustified wrath, that I had grown immune to its sting.

By now she was seething. "No," she said, "I want you to stop holding up my docket. You've got twenty minutes to figure it out."

I signaled to the defendant and his lawyer to meet in the hallway. The defendant seemed scared as he walked out of the courtroom and tried to gather his thoughts. I extended my hand to calm him down. "Sir, my name is Laura Coates. What would you like to tell me? I'm listening." He shook my hand and started to cry, covering my outstretched hand with his other hand as if in prayer.

"We don't have much time . . . the judge said there wasn't that much time," he mumbled. His voice cracked and his eyes blinked rapidly.

His attorney placed his hand on his shoulder. "It's gonna be alright. We're not giving up yet." The word "yet" lingered.

I picked up on his lead, reluctant to appear too sympathetic. I didn't want to give him false hope. "Judges can't tell time, sir. I'll return when I have an answer. Now," I said, with a tinge of exasperation at the prospect of wasting my time, "what's going on?" I wanted to be open-minded but I felt guarded.

He started to speak but kept looking at the crowds in the hallway, nervous that someone might recognize him. His voice trailed off each time someone passed by—he was reluctant to finish if anyone was within earshot. His voice was inaudible over the hallway chatter.

His lawyer spoke up and asked whether we could speak privately. I said that there were no free meeting rooms on the floor—that they were all being used for trial prep. He repeated his client's story but said he really couldn't add much more, and that he was sure his client had not fathered a child. His demeanor outside the courtroom was so muted I wondered if he actually believed his client or whether his advocacy was merely perfunctory.

"How do I know that? Give me something to work with," I implored.

He looked at his client for consent to proceed. I was beginning to get annoyed and hoped there would be some meat on the bone. I had just ticked off a judge with a long memory and a penchant for holding grudges.

The man looked at me, stammering quietly. "She's, any, she, well, that's not my type, miss, but I don't want to get into that here. I don't have girlfriends, you understand. So how could I be accused of beating one up? And a child—I don't have kids. I didn't have sex with her or any woman ever. You understand what I'm saying? No women. I'm . . . well, I'm . . ."

"Gay?" I completed his sentence, immediately reading between the lines. I hoped this was not his only offer of proof. He dropped my hand and stepped back.

His head rose, stunned that I had really said it aloud. He paused for a moment before nodding. "You're not going to say that in the courtroom, right? Like, it's not going to be in some sort of record, right? Right?" he frantically asked his attorney. His attorney shrugged.

"I mean, if it helps, I don't . . ." His attorney reconsidered, turning to me. "Will you tell the court?"

"Tell the court what, exactly? That your client has told me his sexual orientation?" I realized that my tone was more biting that I had intended and would be misconstrued as identical to that of the judge, whose behavior I resented.

I exhaled, my voice immediately softening at the realization, and said to the defendant: "Thank you for sharing that with me. I can tell it wasn't easy and you certainly didn't want to do it under these circumstances. Please understand that I'm not questioning your sexual orientation or trying to be dismissive of it. It's really . . . it's none of my business, personally."

I turned to his lawyer. I didn't see how I could make this my business professionally, either, in the way he needed. "You know that won't be enough. I can't prove that here."

I turned back to the defendant. I didn't want to talk about him as if he wasn't there, so I spoke to him directly again. "Sir, from the judge's standpoint, and mine, standing here right now, there's no way for me to prove that you: a) weren't in a relationship with that woman, b) didn't assault her, and c) didn't father a child with her."

His eyes widened as he jerked his head back. I could almost read his thoughts. First, disbelief that you could be asked to prove your sexuality. Second, concern over how you would actually prove it. Defeat stretched across his brow as he stood rigidly in the hall.

I tried to ease his mind by focusing on what the court needed to know. "I'm not asking you to prove anything to me, other than your actual identity. Look, let's not overcomplicate this. You said the cops were sloppy and never really interviewed you, right? So, let's start at the beginning—how the conversation should've gone in an ideal world. Did you ever see the mug shot for the person they were looking for?

"No."

"You never saw anyone compare you to the photo?"

"No."

"They asked to see your license?"

"Yes."

"The names matched?"

"Yes. I don't have a middle name, though."

"Did they take your height or ask for your address or anything like that?"

"No."

"Did they say anything to you about why you were being arrested?"

"Not really, but everything happened so fast, and I kept telling them I hadn't done anything wrong and was asking them, like, why they were arresting me if I hadn't done anything wrong, and it was crazy, and it all happened so fast . . ." He divulged all this without taking a breath.

I paused for a moment to call the assigned prosecutor. He didn't answer, and his voice mail was full. His email gave an out-of-office automated reply. I wondered if this was one of the federal prosecutors who had recently announced they were leaving the office, but I didn't have time to scan through my emails to find out.

I turned to his lawyer for confirmation that what I was being told was consistent with his understanding. There was nothing in my file to corroborate any of it. He nodded.

"Okay, so let's start with finding out who they were looking for and then see if that's actually you."

I asked him for his license and told him to walk with me to a satellite prosecutors' office, located in the basement of the courthouse to enable prosecutors to prepare for trial and review arrest paperwork with officers before arraignments. When we arrived, I asked him to wait outside with his lawyer. Defendants weren't permitted into the basement office. A courtroom marshal had followed us to the basement and was standing nearby—a gift from the judge still intent on proving a point.

I pushed the door open, shaking my head at the way it had been rigged to prevent it from being locked during the day. I wondered off-handedly what we would do if someone wanted to come inside. If someone was mad enough to barge in, they wouldn't be bringing a box of cookies.

The second I entered the room, the flurry of activity hit me. I stepped over an officer's outstretched legs, almost stumbling as he simultaneously tried to lift them out of the way.

"Ooh, sorry! Did I getcha?" he said.

"It's okay, don't worry about it." I kept moving.

"Anyone had a mistaken identity defendant case before?" I shouted to the room.

The question momentarily paused the commotion, before one officer deadpanned, "Every single arrest."

Laughter erupted as the bustle instantly resumed. I wondered if the defendant on the other side of the door had heard the laughter. I already regretted having asked the question.

Several prosecutors were milling at workstations, preparing for trial. I asked one to move so I could use the computer. "For what?" he said, shoveling a half-eaten sandwich into his mouth. A glob fell onto his pants as he let his irritation be known. "Oh come on! I'm in front of a jury with a fucking stain now, Coates. All because some asshole told you you've got the wrong guy."

"Well, maybe you'll finally dry-clean the suit now. That stain is not the problem. And if you already knew why I needed the computer, you shouldn't have asked. Can you please just move?"

He scooted over six inches but remained seated. I leaned over his armrest and typed quickly. My breast skimmed his arm and he jerked it away. "Didn't mean that—my apologies," he said, suddenly self-conscious.

"And who eats tuna fish before a trial?" I said. "You stink." I was early in my pregnancy and had to suppress the urge to dry-heave.

He sighed and kissed the air as his stench swirled. He winked as he walked away, not self-conscious anymore.

I began searching through the records, unsure both of what I was looking for and what precisely I'd find. I relayed the story to another group of prosecutors preparing for their individual trials. One asked, "Which judge is this in front of?" The group collectively winced at my response and warned me that I was wasting my time and would lose my credibility with the judges if I fell for these stories.

I glanced at the clock: fifteen minutes had already elapsed since I'd left the courtroom. I was sure the judge would be staring at the clock.

"We'd lose more credibility if he's telling the truth. Don't act like cops don't get it wrong sometimes." I cocked my head to underscore the point.

One prosecutor motioned with his eyes toward the uniformed officers within earshot, warning me to be more aware of my surroundings. The prosecutors snickered as they walked away.

I swallowed, wondering which officer I may have just offended. I hoped it wasn't one that I would need on my trial. I quickly looked around to see if anyone met my eyes, but no one did. I felt relieved. Perhaps my mistake of pointing out the truth would go unnoticed.

I returned to the computer, trying to access the mug shots, wondering if this would end up being really as simple as comparing a photograph. I contemplated the odds that it really was the wrong guy and a cursory scan in the courthouse basement could prove it. I chuckled aloud, shaking the scenario out of my mind in disbelief. It would all be too absurd.

Mary, another Black female prosecutor, rolled her litigation bag into the room, noticed my chuckle, and approached me to hear the joke. She was in need of a laugh after the morning she'd had and said so. I reluctantly shared the story, half expecting her to respond like the others but hoping she would understand. She didn't laugh. Instead she turned toward the peanut gallery of officers I had just hoped not to alienate and said, "They often fuck this up. Let me help." That the officers heard. She chided them with lifted brows.

One officer looked at her, removing a headphone from one of his ears. "What do we always fuck up?" he challenged.

"You heard me," she said boldly.

He sucked his teeth and replaced the headphone. They obviously had a history.

"You're gonna have to tell me that story later," I said, intrigued by the tension between them.

"It's a long one," she said, lowering the handle into her rolling briefcase.

Six minutes later, I was watching the printer release a photograph of the right man. He was six inches shorter, fifty pounds heavier, at least three shades darker, and looked nothing like the man who was nervously crying out in the hallway. I walked over to the female prosecutor, now sitting across from the officer she hated and to whom she'd directed her earlier comment.

"You won't believe this," I said, asking her to look at the man in the hallway before showing her the printout.

We looked at each other and shook our heads in mutual disgust.

"Wow . . . what if . . ."

"What if," I ended, and started toward the door to speak with the defendant.

"This was your case?" she asked, prepared to berate me.

"Nope. It's his." I pointed to the name written with a Sharpie on the file.

She forced herself to exhale, opening her lips only slightly as if whistling without sound.

"Oh, you should've told me that from the beginning. I could've told you how he is. Doesn't give a fuck about anything."

"Is he the one—" I asked, recalling the gossip about this prosecutor.

"Yup!" she said. I wondered if we were talking about the same person.

"Wait till I tell . . ." Her cell phone interrupted her plans. "Thank you!" she said. "Jury question! I gotta go."

She turned toward the offending officer, speaking loudly in case he tried to turn up the volume and drown her out. "Some of us are going to go do our jobs right now." She enunciated the last three words. "Some of us actually answer our phones. So we know when to be where we are supposed to be!"

The officer again removed his headphone from one ear, holding it an inch from his face. "Did you say something?" he said, taunting her.

I stepped over his legs on my way back to the hallway, unwilling to stay and see how the play would end.

As I approached the defendant, I saw that he was sitting with his head in his hands, his elbows bouncing on his thighs. I extended my hand again, this time handing him the picture of the right man.

"I guess we all do look alike, huh?" I said.

As the defendant clutched the page, his lawyer touched the corner of it and then stood and turned around in a circle, resting his hands on his hips. I wondered whether there had been a way for him to obtain the photo himself, and, if so, why he hadn't done so sooner. "Really? Really." First dubious and then incredulous. He pulled at his suit jacket as he spoke.

The defendant stared at the picture in disbelief and shook his head. He exhaled for a moment and turned his eyes toward the ceiling. I thought he was about to cry again, when I noticed that his hands, holding either side of the paper, began to crumple its edges. Now he was pissed.

He started to yell at me, obviously frustrated and enraged by the absurdity of the confusion and the anguish that he had endured. As the marshal approached, I held up my hand in protest and signaled his retreat.

"I know you're upset and you'd like someone to yell at. But I'm not the one. You've still got an active warrant on you, and now I've gotta find the right person. Let's go back to the courtroom and inform the judge."

We made our way back to the courtroom in shocked silence. My mind was racing at how easy this had been to clear up, how little effort it had taken. I just couldn't wrap my mind around it.

En route, I called the assigned prosecutor again, giving him another chance to resolve it personally. I checked my email again to see if he had responded to me.

"Can't reach him, huh? I'm telling you, this guy . . ." The attorney shook his head as he reiterated just how unresponsive and unprofessional my colleague had been. I couldn't defend him. There was certainly more than one person to blame.

Upon seeing me enter the courtroom, the judge recalled the case. Before any of us could make our way back to our respective tables within the well of the courtroom, the judge sarcastically asked the defendant, "Well? Are we going to jail today or not, sir?"

"Your Honor," I said, "it seems there has indeed been a mistake."

I approached the skeptical judge as I presented her with the documentation, along with a family court order that acknowledged a different man as the child's father. The judge stared at me with disdain.

"Very well, Ms. Coates. Sir, it seems that you are free to go. Have a good day. I'll quash the warrant with respect to you, but there remains a warrant for the other individual. I'm assuming you'll try to find the right person this time, government? Call the next case," she said, scribbling onto paperwork before handing it to the clerk.

"That's it?" I heard him say. "That was all they needed? That's all it took after all this?"

Remembering his role, his defense attorney spoke up. "Your Honor, you laughed at my client. At the very least, some kind of apology . . ."

The judge interrupted him, turned to me, and expectantly asked, with raised eyebrows, "Ms. Coates?"

"Yes, Your Honor?" I retorted.

"He's owed an apology," she said, impatiently gesturing with one palm face-up, the index finger of her other hand wrapped around her pen. She cocked her head to one side with delight as a smirk subtly reached the left corner of her mouth, dying to spread into a full shit-eating grin.

Indignant, I begged her pardon. I was irritated not just because the judge did not apologize for her own unprofessionalism but because of the role she had played in this man's mistreatment. I was irritated by her demand for other reasons. She knew full well the implications of a federal prosecutor's acknowledging any form of misconduct and the potential civil exposure that might create for the department, albeit perhaps justified. I considered belaboring our stalemate, but my ego deferred to the fact that while I was not personally to blame, the United States had wronged this man, and he deserved an apology.

So, this Black woman turned to the Black man who was deserving of that apology and said, "Sir, I am very sorry for what you had to experience, not just today but before today. I'm sorry that no one listened to you or took the time to perform even a cursory inspection of those photographs. You're obviously not the man who the warrant squad was looking for, and you should not be here today answering for his crime. I'm sorry. The United States apologizes for any inconvenience."

I instantly regretted my word choice. "Inconvenience" was a gross understatement and I knew better.

"Excuse me, not just inconvenience," I said. "That wasn't the right word to use. It doesn't cover it. It never should have happened. To you. Or anyone."

He bobbed his head at me as if taking stock of my words. He shook his head at the judge, snorted, and looked down. He exhaled loudly and placed his hands on the table in front of him, tapping it twice with his left knuckles before gripping it as if he were about to upend it. You could hear his fingernails clawing the underside. He released his grip and started out of the courtroom.

He paused as he passed my table and pointed at me.

"That, that . . ." Clearly he was torn between choosing his words and mincing them. "That shouldn't have come from you." He pounded once on my desk and stormed out of the courtroom as the judge spoke.

"I guess the exception proved the rule today. You must be proud of yourself, Ms. Coates," the judge half-heartedly offered.

This time, it was my turn to guffaw. "Proud, Your Honor?" I frowned. "No one should be proud of what happened here today. But just out of curiosity, which part did you think was the exception and which part the rule?"

The clerk stole a quick glance at the judge.

The judge stonily commanded her to call the next case as we held each other's eyes.

I expected the next four defendants to claim misidentification through their counsel, if only in jest. Instead, each of the four Black defendants who had been sitting inside the courtroom when the apology was issued stopped to nod at me when they walked to their table. I understood the meaning. They knew who I was. And who I was not.

6

A Seat at the (Right) Table

*On the Tension Between Black Defense
Attorneys and Prosecutors*

"Can I ask you something?"

I looked up from my plate mid-bite to find a Black woman around my age staring at me, her head cocked to the side.

I recognized her from the courthouse. She was a defense attorney, and a fearsome one at that. We'd yet to try a case together, but her reputation preceded her. Her name was Shawna. I wondered what she wanted.

"Of course. What's on your mind?" I was genuinely intrigued.

"Why are you a prosecutor?" She squinted and lifted her chin.

"Why am I a prosecutor?" I repeated as I put down my fork.

"Yes, seriously. Why are you a prosecutor?" she asked again, nodding with each word.

"Why do you ask?" I probed, returning her squint, wagging my head.

"Just curious, is all."

"Well, why are you a defense attorney?" I asked. My response was admittedly sophomoric.

"That's an easier answer. Yours, I bet, isn't."

"You think so, huh?"

"I do. It doesn't fit. I've seen you in court. You don't hate the defendants."

"I didn't know that was required," I said, rolling my head and laughing before I looked back at her. From my seated position, her stature filled the room.

"It seems like . . . can I sit down?" She pulled a chair from the next table along the floor as she asked. I nodded, sitting back against my chair to add distance. I had purposely chosen the table for one in the basement of a small cafe. It had become a habit to grab lunch upstairs amid the bustling crowd and then retreat in peace to dine in the basement.

She continued, "It seems like your office is the kind of place the White boys who got picked last in gym class go to play God. Know what I mean?" She tilted her head and scrunched up her nose, exposing her top gumline. "You're not that. I'm surprised you'd be one of them." Her gums were still exposed as she waited for a response.

I took a bite of my salad, swallowing part of it as I said, "I'm guessing someone in my office pissed you off today, huh?" I swallowed the rest down with a smile.

"Eh, they piss me off every day. Not just today. But seriously—" She looked around the room, studying its ambience with down-turned lips. "I hardly come down here. The koi pond is a nice but random touch, don't you think? It's too quiet for me." The koi pond was unexpected but went with the theme. Now, the silence. The silence was precisely why I came.

"Why does it surprise you that I'm a prosecutor?" I picked up the conversation, curious to see which assumptions she had already made.

"Um . . . because you're a Black woman?" She pretended to be answering a softball question in a pop quiz. "And you see how your office is. Doesn't it bother you? I don't know. I couldn't do it." She frowned as she leaned back dramatically.

I crossed my arms, ambivalent about her tone. She continued through chews of a salted chocolate chip cookie she'd bought upstairs. "Where are you from? Did I hear Minnesota? That might explain some things."

"Here we go," I said. "What do you think it explains?"

"Oh, no offense, it's just an observation." She squinted again, tilting her head in the other direction as she chewed. Her personality had the shelf life of unrefrigerated dairy.

"Actually, it's not just an observation, but let me make some of my own," I countered. "You're obviously accustomed to insulting people and getting away with it. So, let's see . . . is this the part where insecure people squirm and try to get you to like them? Or is that coming after a few more insults?"

"Oh no, I've offended you." She was more flippant than sincere. She bit her thumbnail instead of her cookie before rubbing the spit off with her index finger.

"No, but I'm wondering why that seems to be your intention. To offend me."

"Let's start over. I didn't even introduce myself."

"I know who you are, and you seem to already know a little bit about me. Or at least you think you do. You got the Minnesota part right."

"We got off on the wrong foot. I'll admit, that's my fault. But I am genuinely curious about you. I've always wondered what makes someone want to be a prosecutor."

I was increasingly agitated by her condescension. "And I'm sure you've had plenty of people to ask. But here you are suddenly curious because it's me. Were there more pretend questions in this interview or . . ." I allowed my disinterest to fill the air.

"It's Laura, right?"

"Really?" I cocked my head, exhausted by the useless repartee.

"Okay, lemme stop. You got me. I'll stop." She held up her hands in surrender. She mimed waving a flag. Now I knew I didn't like her. "I just have to get this off my chest, because I always wonder. You know these cops are dirty, right? You know that. So why would you help them? And please don't tell me justice."

"That's exactly what I'm going to tell you. Justice. You don't think justice is an acceptable reason?"

"I just think it's a cliché answer. Canned."

"Okay, well, at least you got it off your chest."

"So you think you're doin' the right thing?" she continued.

"Why do you get to decide whether I'm doing the right thing or not?" I was annoyed that I kept responding to her. "I really don't need to explain myself to you, but I am surprised you don't think the victims are entitled to justice. On account of many of them also being Black women."

"Interesting. So it's about the victims for you?"

"Can you think of a better reason?"

"Yes. Well, no. I mean, it's a good answer."

"Are you always this patronizing?"

"No. Well, yes," she winked.

"You know, it's funny. You seem to get off on trying to make people uncomfortable," I observed. "You're very . . . reactive. For someone who likes power so much, you're not really in a position to wield any."

"I'm not?"

"No. As defense, you can only react to power. You can try to call the reaction strategy, but it's really only a reflex. Like a hammer on your knee."

She tried to hide her grimace by squinting one eye. She deflecting, asking, "And you have power? Like a White boy in gym class after all."

"No, not me," I said, holding the fingerhole of my mug as I sipped. "I just understand the value in being the decision maker rather than having to deal with someone else's decision. You gotta admit: it would feel nice sometimes to get justice by preventing an injustice."

"Oh, so you're the Trojan horse."

"You're really hoping to find an analogy that will actually work, aren't you?" At this point I was tickled by her determination to categorize me.

"I'm trying to figure you out."

"Why?"

"Because I can't understand you."

"Okay . . . ," I said, indifferent to her need. I hoped she would leave. "Look. I come down here to relax. I actually like the silence after the lunch-hour rush. You must have somewhere to be, right? A verdict or a motion you gotta run to? Hopefully . . ."

"You don't think I have any power?" She was apparently in no rush to leave. "We do have power—my office just doesn't abuse it like you people do."

"And, just so we're clear, who's the 'you people' in this scenario?"

"Excuse me . . . prosecutors."

"And how do we abuse the power exactly? Should I stop prosecuting rape cases this week?" I glanced toward my rolling briefcase. "Too abusive?"

"You know I'm not talking about those cases."

"Honestly, I don't know what you're talking about, and I'm not even sure you do, either."

"Drug cases. You really can stomach those? I believe your office calls them—let me get this right—'victimless crimes,' right?"

"And here I was just trying to stomach this conversation." I continued eating my food, ready to block her out.

She leaned back, pressing the back of her hand against her lips before she spoke. "Look, I think we got off to the wrong start."

"You mentioned that already." I kept chewing.

"I bet you switch sides one day, sis."

"You think so, huh?" I swiped my tongue across my upper canine to clear a piece of lettuce that, like her, refused to get lost.

"I do. You won't be able to stomach what you're going to see for very long." I wondered why she was acting like I was a novice. I had been a lawyer longer than she had. "Once you realize you're on the wrong side. And I won't even give you a hard time when you apply to my office. You can even use me as a reference. I'll supervise your first trial. Give you constructive feedback." She bobbed her head at the word "constructive."

"A reference? Really." Her arrogance was as astounding as it was contrived. I sipped the rest of my water through my straw.

"Twenty bucks says I'm right."

"If I pay you twenty dollars right now, can we never have this conversation again?" I wiped my mouth with my napkin and tossed it on my plate. I let out a yawn.

I hoped she would finally get up to leave. She nibbled on her cookie instead, turning her head toward the koi pond, noting, "I was wrong. It is nice down here. I can see why you like the peace."

"It *was* peaceful, yes." I shook my head at her refusal to heed my social cues. "You don't really take hints well, huh?"

"We're not enemies, you know."

"I know that. Do you? The way you came at me makes me think

you don't. It seems like you've been rehearsing some kind of 'martinis with your enemies' scene here."

"No, I know that. I know we're not enemies, I mean. I do." She looked down for a second. "I'm gonna lose my case today, you know."

I waited.

"One of your White boys from gym class really pulled a number on me. I told this guy's family . . . I told him . . . that we could win this one. The jury . . . well . . . the jury wasn't on his side. He's young. I'm not going to be able to get him out of it."

I nodded.

"You don't know what it's like, do you? I mean, after the verdict. You never go back there to watch the reaction. When you have to feed them some line about it not being over yet. We can still appeal!" she pantomimed. "When they're younger than you. Or worse, the same age."

I studied her face and brushed a crumb off the side of the table. "What's his name?"

"Who? The White boy from gym class?"

"No, the man you're going to convince it's not over yet. I'm guessing he's the reason you're in need of a punching bag."

"Is that what you think I'm doing?" She looked genuinely disappointed by my assessment. "Joseph. His name is Joseph."

"And how will you explain it to Joseph?"

"I don't know. Maybe I'll tell him it's about justice," she snapped. I finished my last swig of water and let it hit the table like a gavel. I pulled my purse over my shoulder and slid back.

"I'm sorry. I didn't. I'm sorry." She touched my forearm. "Please sit, I mean stay. Please stay. This was your table. I'm sorry. You were just being nice to ask. I fucked up the moment. Sorry."

I wondered how often she got in her own way. And how she presented to a jury.

I remained standing, no longer interested in her story. Even though I realized it was a projection, this was the last snide remark I would hear. I was done prolonging the conversation for the sake of being polite.

I stared at her hand on my arm. She let go and nodded. She looked at the orange speckled fish circling the water display as I put my plate in the table busser's bin.

Her phone vibrated, and she gazed at it for a moment before answering.

"I'll be right there. Thank you," she said calmly.

"Verdict's in?" I asked, sliding on my coat.

"Verdict is in," she confirmed, and began to gather herself to stand.

"What's it like for you?" she asked, this time without pretense. "When you lose, I mean. Be honest."

"Painful," I said. "We have the same conversation with the victim that you have with Joseph. Only there's no hope for an appeal. It really is over for them. It's just a different kind of prison."

She nodded, tossing her coat over her forearm as she hoisted her bag over her shoulder.

"Twenty bucks. Don't forget. You know I'm right." She wagged her finger at me.

"Don't hold your breath," I said, smiling.

She turned on her heel, disappearing up the stairs to tell Joseph it was not over yet.

7

Babyface

*On the Conviction of a Baby-Faced Defendant
Who Acts Against His Self-Interest*

The name Lawrence didn't seem to suit him. He had a baby face, and the description quickly became my moniker for him. It seemed I was not the only one to focus on his youthful appearance. In fact, the judge asked his attorney his age no fewer than three times during each of our pretrial hearings, to the point where the attorney asked to see a copy of his license so that he could show the judge that "Babyface" was, in fact, no longer a teenager. Babyface didn't look a single minute over thirteen. The judge's query was more than mere curiosity.

In the District of Columbia, judges have the discretion to sentence a convicted defendant as a so-called youthful offender. That classification not only offered probation instead of incarceration, it also permitted the defendant to ultimately expunge their record for that particular crime. Frankly, it recognized a youthful indiscretion and offered a second chance. But at the time, the second chance was only offered to defendants who were *under* the age of twenty-two.

That's why birthdays aren't always cause for celebration, certainly not in a justice system that arbitrarily decided the cutoff for youth. At twenty-one, Lawrence had been arrested for illegally possessing a gun, a felony. In spite of having confessed to the crime, he refused to plead guilty. He refused, even with the knowledge that he would turn twenty-two by the trial, aging him out of the classification of a youthful offender. Instead, he exercised his right to a trial.

And today was the first and only day of that trial. And also the first time the judge did not inquire about Babyface's age. Yet here he was, poised to be tried for possession of an illegal, loaded firearm, seized following a high-speed police chase through the streets of Washington, D.C. Two other people were in the car: his twenty-year-old naive-looking girlfriend in braces with law textbooks in her backpack sitting in the front passenger seat, and a thirty-something man seated in the back whose rap sheet began before the baby-faced defendant with no record was out of elementary school.

So imagine my surprise when I was initially assigned the case and learned that the defendant had told the officers that the gun belonged to him. Naturally, I thought, he must have been strong-armed by his passenger, Trevor, into taking the heat. I demanded to see the videotaped confession. He had indeed confessed. In detail. He had even described the gun. In fact, he had been so eager to talk to the officers that I wondered if he understood that he was a suspect. Meanwhile, Trevor remained silent in a vidcotaped interview. The two then were placed in the same holding cell. They never spoke, but witnesses said Babyface tried to get the attention of his friend.

I'll admit, he was adorable, with the face of a toddler, elongated. He smiled nervously and chewed on his fingernails, abruptly catching himself—perhaps remembering his mother's orders to stop? He folded his arms and buried his fists under his biceps as if to restrain himself from this compulsion . . . only to retrieve those fists moments later to begin the gnawing again. His lower jaw moved side to side as he ground the gnawed nail between his front teeth, holding the remnant still while his mouth formed around it to respond to his attorney.

When he wasn't biting his nails, he repeatedly pinched his tie knot, nervously confirming its closure before flipping the end of the tie back and forth to reveal its underside playfully. He bounced his heel up and down in his black lace-up dress shoe while pulling up an oversized sock with a persistent slouch, and I wondered to whom the socks really belonged. His white button-down shirt was transparent enough to reveal the prominent outline of a ribbed white tank top underneath. His suit jacket was folded over the back of the bench. I watched as he moved it to the other side of his girlfriend sitting beside him, holding it delicately as if it were crepe paper. She looked nervous, pensively listening to Babyface's attorney's words.

In person, Babyface looked different from his arrest photo. The hair that once coiled into vertical twists about his crown was now shaved low, drawing attention to his already pronounced cheekbones. His freckles were suddenly abundant, no longer hidden under patches of facial hair unwilling to connect into a semblance of a beard. Unsmiling in the photo, he had lifted his eyebrows and chin in an attempt to appear equal parts defiant, irreverent, and nonchalant—a curious combination for one intending to profess his innocence.

Here in court, too, his eyebrows were lifted, now above the black frames of an ill-fitting pair of glasses, undoubtedly an accessory his lawyer counseled would render him more distinguished. They slid down his face, his minimal bridge failing to hold them in place, as he listened to his attorney's whispers. He periodically lifted and then replaced them in front of his eyes, comparing his perspective with and then without the glasses like a child experimenting by looking through a pair of sunglasses.

A man stood hunched over the back of the defendant's bench. He was leaning his elbows on Babyface's jacket, using it as a cushion against the wood. Babyface glanced at the wrinkles forming on the jacket, but looked away rather than address it.

His expressions alternated between concern and surprise as he listened intently to his lawyer. He would smile and blink profusely to demonstrate his understanding each time she paused, as if he had taken a course in active listening. I watched them talk from my perch on a bench toward the back of the courtroom as we all waited for the jury to return from lunch. I was eager to hear whether the defense intended to present its case, when suddenly their body language suggested they had reached a conclusion. I looked down at my phone to check the time.

His attorney swiveled her head, searching behind her, with her elbow jutting over the back of the bench. She waved at me when she spotted me behind her, mouthing the word "talk," jerking her head toward the hall. I turned to look at the clock. The jury was due back in just shy of twenty minutes. I nodded, motioning toward the meeting rooms between the double doors of the courtroom entrance. As she slid her glasses to the top of her head like a headband restraining her hair, she rose but motioned to her client to stay seated. The man with the familiar face sat down beside the defendant, taking the attorney's seat in her absence.

She smiled as she approached, suddenly aware of the need to explain the sudden request to speak mid-trial. I'd had so many cases with this counsel, and she was always on the brink of pissing you off with her last-minute shenanigans. I assumed this would be no different. My acid reflux was always relentless during trial, and I was in no mood to prolong it.

"You know I'm not offering him a plea, right?" I said, initiating the conversation and scoffing preemptively. She knew that our office's policy toward plea offers was firm: there would be no better offer than the pre-indictment offer. The next-best offer from the Department of Justice would be the one after the grand jury indictment but before we readied for trial. So today, on the day of trial, the only option would be to plead guilty to the full indictment. All charges. No exceptions. Any lesser plea after I had greeted the jury wouldn't be entertained. Besides, I had already more than proven my case.

"Not asking for a plea," she retorted, trying to catch me off guard.

"Okay . . . how can I help you, then?" I rubbed my décolletage in vain as the acid burned through my chest cavity, with an uncomfortable film forming on my tongue.

"I need immunity," she said, holding up her hands to insist on my patience. "Hear me out. I have a witness who says the gun is his. The backseat passenger. He says it's his gun."

"Really," I said, with feigned incredulity. "And who is this wonderful person? Let me guess: Trevor?" I took a swig from my bottle of ginger ale to relieve the burning.

"I know what you're thinking, Laura," she said, fully engaged, aware that we were now sixteen minutes from the jury's return.

"Really," I repeated, this time amused. "Tell me what you think I'm thinking."

"Why haven't I told you this before? Why am I just telling you now?" she asked, articulating the obvious without yet providing the response. I waited for one, already confident it would be wholly lacking. She continued, "I only just found out about this. His attorney is here, and Trevor wants immunity before he'll testify that it's really his gun."

"Alright, I'll play . . . for now." I shook my head. "Where is his attorney? And where is Trevor—who, by the way, was already questioned by the police following his own arrest, right after your client confessed, on videotape. You remember that part of trial, right?"

"I know. I know. I know. I know. But just hear him out. If, after you hear his story, you want to pass, I'll ask the judge to do a little prodding. Doesn't hurt to ask. I can't very well put on a defense without him, right?"

"I'll hear what he has to say as long as his lawyer is here."

"Right, of course. One sec, I'll grab him."

I waited, and used the opportunity to fumble through my purse for anything that would relieve the burning in my chest. I unscrewed my bottle of ginger ale again and had only begun to drink from it when she returned with another defense attorney and his client in tow. I recognized him as the man ruining the defendant's jacket and also from the recorded police interview. I took my time drinking from the bottle as they milled around the room, remaining in my seat as I lightly put the bottle cap back in place, allowing it to teeter for a moment while I swallowed.

I twisted the cap tightly as Trevor's lawyer apologized for his client's belated attack of conscience. I turned to Babyface's attorney. "Oh, you can go. I'll follow up with you when I'm done."

She lingered, not accustomed to being dismissed.

"I assume you already know what he's gonna say, right? One of us has to be in the courtroom when the judge returns. I nominate you."

"You'll let me know?" she asked.

"Of course—oh wait, you were talking to his attorney." Having realized this, I turned to Trevor's lawyer, adding, "Will you let her know, please?"

He laughed, agreeing. "Yes. Give us a minute."

She left, closing the door behind her. Trevor's lawyer turned to me. "Now you know me—I don't do these kinds of eleventh-hour tricks."

"Is this a trick?" I said, honing in on his intent. "I already know it's the eleventh hour."

"No, no trick," he said, shaking his head. He explained that his client wanted to do the right thing, to come clean. It was his gun, and he didn't want his friend to take the rap for it. The word "friend" lingered in the air. The baby-faced defendant sitting on trial waiting for his lawyer to return looked like he could be the friend of this man's child, not his own.

"Oh, you're his friend?" I asked, turning to Trevor, each word delivered in rapid staccato.

"Yes, my friend," Trevor replied slowly, in tune with my skepticism.

"His friend," I repeated, this time a statement. "Are you aware that your friend has been sitting through trial all day? Were you unaware of any of the prior court dates leading up to trial or when he was offered a chance to plead guilty before trial? Any of those times that might have helped your friend before now—in the middle of trial?"

Trevor was as condescending as he was tickled by my panache, laughing after each question. He ignored the questions and described how he wanted to testify in Babyface's defense. He was prepared to testify that it was his gun, and that Babyface was taking the rap for him to improve his street cred. Babyface wasn't from around the neighborhood. In fact, he grew up in a stable, two-parent home, surrounded by grandparents, aunts, uncles, and cousins on both sides. He had never been in trouble before, but he had gotten involved with Trevor because he wanted to fit in with his circle for some unknown reason. Trevor said he had told him to say that the gun was his, and had convinced Babyface that the police would just give him a slap on the wrist. Worst-case scenario, Trevor believed, he could get a "juvie sentence" because Babyface wasn't even twenty-one yet.

"He's twenty-two," I corrected him.

"Nah, you sure?"

"Yes," his lawyer and I said in unison. "He just turned twenty-two." I said.

"Really? Well, whatever, I thought he was younger than that. Twenty-two, then. Well, look, I told him it wouldn't be a problem. He's a good kid. I mean, he's not from around my way. I keep telling him not to mess with those folks. Stay where you are. I'm not even trying to be here."

"But you're there," I said, stating the obvious. "Why not leave?"

"Easier said than done." He smirked. "You gotta have the means to leave, right? It's not just, like, a matter of want. It's about financial means," he said, emphasizing "financial" as if to demonstrate the depth of his vocabulary.

"Did you tell him what the gun looked like?" I asked.

"No. I just said to say it was his."

"Didn't you think the detective would ask him to describe it?"

"No."

"Well, he did."

"But I never showed it to him. He didn't even see it. I just put it in his bag when they pulled us over."

"Funny. He described the make, model, and color. Said the kind of bullets. The number of bullets."

"He made it up."

"You mean to tell me he guessed the right answer to a question he didn't know he'd be asked?"

"Yeah, I mean, it's a regular type of gun. People have it. He must have just guessed. Damn. I can't believe he got it right, though. Look. It's not his gun. It's mine. I'll testify to that. I can't let him go down for me. It wouldn't be right."

"Why the sudden conscience? The trial was scheduled a few

months ago. Why only come forward now? It's hard to believe a man with immunity. Maybe if you'd had something to lose."

"Why would I ever talk to you without immunity? I know my rights. You could have dropped his charges and then charged me instead. The judge would have revoked my probation and I would have been sent back. The arrest alone almost got me sent back. Any other time, the cops don't believe a word any of us say, but this time, suddenly, you're telling me the detective just believed him. Why do you even care about this case? You really need a win that bad?"

"I don't actually need a win at all, but it sounds like you do." I stared at him, studying him as if it were a pure first impression. "What kind of gun was it? Answer without looking at your attorney."

"I don't know."

"What color was it?

"I don't know. Black . . . silver . . . like a blackish silver."

His answers were wrong, but I didn't risk revealing that to him for fear of inadvertently prepping him for trial. He would have to testify about what he actually knew or pretended to know, not what I helped him become aware of.

"Bullets?"

"Was it loaded? I don't know." I had just told him about the bullets moments before. He wasn't a quick study.

"You said you put the gun inside of his bag? What did the bag look like?"

"A black backpack? Yeah, a backpack with two straps." It was a messenger bag with writing on it and one long strap.

"What color?"

"I don't even know. But it had to be black." It was orange.

"How did you get inside of the bag? Was it zipped?"

"I must have. That's the only way you can get into a backpack, so yeah." It had two buckles.

"Where was the bag?"

"I don't know." It was in the trunk. The locked trunk.

"When did you tell him to lie for you?"

"In the car."

"Did you ever see him touch the gun?"

"No." His DNA was on the gun.

I had no doubt he was lying, and wondered how much thought Babyface's lawyer had given to putting Trevor on the stand. I called her back inside.

"Well, he's free to testify. I can't stop you," I said, turning to her. "It won't help. You know that." The jury had already heard the evidence of how the gun was found, had seen photographs of the messenger bag, watched the videotaped confession.

"You don't know that," she said. But Trevor's lawyer agreed with me, judging by the look in his eyes.

I checked the clock; the jury would be arriving momentarily. "No," I said, making my decision known. "I'm not going to volunteer immunity. I don't believe him. You're welcome to argue your case to the judge about your inability to mount a defense. If he instructs, I'll consider it."

"Fair enough," she said, clapping her hands together as she followed me back to the courtroom.

"What'd she say?" Babyface asked his attorney, as he shifted his gaze from me to her.

"It's what we thought. We'll approach the judge." He returned his hand to his mouth and resumed gnawing on the outside edge of his pinky nail before yanking his hand down into his lap and sitting on it again. He was wearing his suit jacket now, rubbing the sleeves, trying unsuccessfully to release the wrinkles.

The judge entered the room, reclaiming his seat. "Any matters to address before I recall the jury?" he asked out of sheer habit.

"Yes, Your Honor," defense counsel said immediately. "May we approach?"

The judge leaned in eagerly as we drew near, pushing the white noise button to mask our voices as defense counsel pleaded for the court's intervention.

"I can't mount a defense without that witness, Your Honor. And the government refuses to extend immunity."

"Why can't you grant immunity, government?"

"Because I don't believe him, Your Honor," I said matter-of-factly, already aware where this conversation would lead. I knew he'd try to force my hand, and I wanted my position on the record.

"Call your office. Speak with your supervisor about a letter of immunity request. I've been down this road before and I already know you can't volunteer it on your own at trial. Let's not open this up for an appeal," he said, already betting on a conviction.

We all understood the conundrum. Trevor's lawyer had laid an eleventh-hour trap at Babyface's attorney's request. If I gave Trevor immunity, his testimony could undermine my case and lead to Babyface's acquittal. If I did not give him immunity, and Babyface was convicted, Babyface's attorney would argue on appeal that my decision not to immunize Trevor precluded a meaningful defense and would possibly lead an appellate court to overturn the conviction. If I dismissed the case against Babyface and instead prosecuted Trevor for the crime, Trevor would undoubtedly be able to sow enough doubt of his own guilt by pointing to Babyface's police confession. If Trevor were acquitted for the crime, we couldn't very well attempt to try Babyface again. Not only did we have to contend with double jeopardy, Babyface could now use the government's presentation of evidence against Trevor in his own defense.

"Now?" I asked through a smiling sneer. I recognized their attempt at checkmate.

"Now," the judge commanded, returning my expression with a knowing nod. "I'm not recalling the jury without a witness."

I knew it was likely an empty threat. He wasn't going to delay the trial indefinitely but I indulged his urgency nonetheless.

I retreated to the same meeting room where I had heard from Trevor just moments ago, and faced the firing squad I was expecting from my supervisor. I held the phone away from my ear as he barked a response. I interjected intermittently to offer that it was the judge's request . . . that I wasn't calling him as a witness . . . yes, I understood why we don't hand out immunity like candy . . . no, this wouldn't be the kind that required a sign-off from the attorney general . . . this wouldn't make our office look bad . . . and of course I had already carried my burden of proof, but it would present an issue on appeal . . . and yes, I'm aware that we'll talk about this the second I return to the office, even with a conviction.

"You do realize if you don't win this case, every defendant will use this tactic against you," he said, referring to the eleventh-hour request for immunity. "You know that, right? Against all of us. Can you win? Huh?" he asked, with annoyed exasperation.

"Yes. The right man is on trial. But I gotta be honest with you. The man's a kid. If his lawyer's smart, which she is, she'll have enough to plant more than a seed of doubt. She'll make it seem like we're going forward in the face of another man's confession only to save face. You and I know that's not what's happening, but I can't guarantee the jury will get that."

"Juries are unpredictable," he said, contemplating.

"Plus, and I know this is a stretch. What if . . ."

"Please don't tell me you actually think this guy didn't do it." He sounded exasperated at the benefit of the doubt I seemed to be extending to Babyface. "Please don't tell me that."

"No, I'm not saying that. He confessed. He definitely confessed.

What I'm saying is, what I mean is, what if he lied during his confession? I know it's a stretch—there are too many coincidences, and their stories don't match. But I mean, what if, for whatever reason, he lied then but is telling the truth now about it not being his?"

"Is he arguing that?"

"Look, we're at trial, so he says he's innocent. We've always been up-front with the jury that there was a passenger—Trevor. His attorney's opening statement didn't fully preview his defense, but I'm assuming he'll argue that it's the passenger's gun. I mean, what else could he do after his confession? If he takes the stand, I'm sure that's what he'll say. And there's no reason he wouldn't take the stand after he's got a witness saying it wasn't even his gun. He's got no priors, so it's not like I can give the jury a reason not to believe him based on any convictions."

"So what do you wanna do?"

"With a confession, I can't dismiss the case. But—and I already know what you're going to say, believe me—I want to give him a fighting chance. I've met my burden, I've proved the case against him. But something about him seems—how can I put it? Seems off."

"Is there a competency issue, because that's a different—"

"No, it's not competency. He seems like he's too silly to make the right choices. Just judging from the company he keeps."

"You just described every other defendant in that courthouse."

"I suppose you're right. Look, you're gonna call me naive. And I already know you're going to clown me for this one, but I'm going to give him a chance here. If the jury believes him, so be it. I'll take the loss on this one."

"*You'll* take the loss? How very kind of you . . . ," he said sarcastically.

"I know it's the office's loss, but I'm just saying. I can't prevent their defense. Let's see what he does. I'll cross the passenger and point out how he's only doing this now that he has immunity and can't be trusted. You know I'll be effective. The jury will do with it what they will, and then it's up to the defendant to testify. I'll give him a letter of immunity for now—it won't affect anything else we've presented to the jury."

I excused myself to go to the prosecutors' office in the basement and printed out a letter that outlined the narrow terms of Trevor's immunity. We wouldn't be able to use whatever he said in trial today against him if we decided to charge him with illegal gun possession. I returned to the courtroom to find an expectant judge summoning opposing counsel and me to the bench.

"Well?" he asked over bifocals, pushing the white noise button again. "We got immunity or not? I'm assuming it's limited just to this case."

"Yes, limited immunity," I confirmed.

"Fine. Recall the jury," he instructed the clerk.

Trevor nodded at me as he walked by to approach the stand. I expected his face to be lopsided, with a smirk, but instead he seemed pensive, deceptively so. As the defense counsel questioned him, he repeated what he had told me earlier. A few of the jurors turned to stare at my profile, furrowing their brows as they wondered at my thoughts. Several exchanged glances, as if to ask why we were not prosecuting him instead of Babyface. Sitting at the prosecutor's table, I fixed my gaze on Trevor, turning my body slightly toward the jury box to show the full complexity of my reaction. I pursed my lips, my eyebrows raised in evident disbelief, the left eyebrow held in position by my middle and index fingers as I tilted my head into my left hand with my elbow positioned on the armrest.

The jurors shifted uncomfortably as Trevor admitted that the gun was his. One juror threw up his hands as if to say, *Why are we here, then?* The judge admonished the juror not to gesticulate.

The defendant's lawyer asked, "Why didn't you tell the police what you're telling us now?"

"They never asked me."

"They never bothered to ask you," she said in a confirmatory tone, nodding while searching the jurors' eyes for sympathy.

"Why now? Why are you telling us this now?" she continued.

"It's the right thing to do. It's just the right thing to do," he said. Neither of them addressed his immunity. This was odd. I assumed that she would have brought up the deal, if only to steal the thunder of my cross-examination. Instead, she turned to the jurors, paraphrasing the testimony emphatically. "He wanted to do the right thing for his friend." She lingered for a moment near the jury box before walking back to her desk. She waited until she sat down to say, "Thank you."

"Thank you," I said, still seated. Trevor's attorney looked at the judge, expecting an instruction for me to stand. I leaned back in my chair, hands folded as if at my leisure.

I pretended to look at my notes, sliding my finger along the words of a sentence I spoke aloud: "He Wanted. To. Do. The. Right. Thing . . . ," I read aloud, still sitting at my desk. "Did I get that quote right?"

"Yeah. That's right," he responded, cocking his head to the side. He faced the jury and said: "I wanted to do the right thing."

"And, uh . . . you didn't say anything to the police before because no one ever asked you. I got that right?"

I rose, careful not to let the speed with which I acted reveal my emotions. If I stood too quickly, my haste could be interpreted as fear. If I stood too slowly, I would seem uncertain of how to deflate their argument.

"Yes," he said, squinting. He leaned forward with his elbows on his thighs, rubbing his palms together. The sound of his palms brushing together reverberated, amplified by the microphone in front of him.

"It's not because you invoked your right to silence before they could ask you anything?" I didn't wait for the answer. "And there's that thing called immunity . . . ," I said, as if asking a question.

He cocked his head to the other side as the jury shifted toward me with interest.

"Immunity. That's what you asked for before you would testify here today, right? In fact, you only asked for it a few moments ago, and you weren't willing to testify without it. Because you wanted to do the right thing?"

"Yes. Why would I testify without it? So you could lock me up instead?" He laughed, rolling his eyes and pointing at me while he looked at the jury. "You're really funny," he said.

The jury didn't laugh.

I used his sarcasm to my advantage. "Well, that wouldn't feel right to you, of course, being locked up for what you say you did . . ." I left just enough room for effect but no answer. "And of course you say it's your gun . . ."

"Yes, my gun."

"A Glock . . . ?"

"Yes." Wrong answer.

"All black . . ."

"Yes." Wrong answer.

"And you put it in his backpack . . ."

"Yup." Wrong answer.

"Under the back of the front seat . . . ?"

"Yes." Wrong answer.

"And you told him to say it was his . . . while you were in the car?"

"Yes." Not according to the testimony of the other passenger, the defendant's girlfriend.

I again marveled at why they hadn't prepped him to give him the benefit of the prior testimony that contradicted his own. The jurors had seen the gun, the messenger bag in which it was found, the photograph of its location inside the trunk. Why risk letting him give the wrong answers now? He could have been sitting in the courtroom this morning or reviewed the paperwork. It was all there. But I couldn't risk assuming that the jury recalled the specific details of my case—this was no time to be unwilling to ask one question too many.

"It's a wonder all of your answers are exactly wrong. They don't match the descriptions in the evidence or any of the paperwork or anything the jury has heard. So you didn't review anything before your attack of conscience, right? If only to get your stories straight?" I said, as I walked past the jury toward my seat.

"Objection!"

I swiveled for effect as I sat down. "Oh, no need. No further questions, Your Honor."

I glanced at the jury as I sat down to assess their impression of Trevor, and discovered ambivalence. The jurors exchanged glances, but their eyes lingered on my face. Aware of the attention, I prolonged the impression. I picked up the pitcher of water before me and slowly poured water into a cup. I placed my elbow down on the table as I poured to ensure that my hand wouldn't inadvertently shake, while conveying my exhaustion with the time spent on having to address his lies. I took a sip, shaking my head to underscore my refusal to even entertain his testimony.

Trevor stepped down from the stand, adjusting the edge of his sweater to reveal the branded emblem on his belt. He nodded in the direction of the defendant, who appeared as eager as a lap dog to receive this attention. Trevor scratched the top of his own head as he passed me, looking down as he walked out toward the back of the courtroom.

"Any other witnesses?" the judge asked, to which the defendant's lawyer called his name.

I watched as Babyface stood up to take the stand. His attorney fixed her client's tie and smoothed the wrinkles on his sleeve. She nodded approvingly, like a mother preparing her son for school pictures. I turned to see the effect the moment had on the jury. One woman smiled endearingly and cast an eye toward me with scorn. I softened my expression from wary to expectant.

As he spoke, it was obvious that his boyish charm had opened doors and disarmed skeptics in other arenas. The jury leaned in while he spoke, attuned to his perceived vulnerability. His quiet demeanor was the foil to Trevor's confidence. It made him sympathetic. From the moment he took the stand, the jury seemed to implore him to confirm that he had simply fallen victim to Trevor's manipulation. His attorney gave him the opportunity.

"Now, Lawrence," she began, with a maternal tone. "Tell us . . . whose gun was it?" She interlaced her fingers and rested her hands on the base of her stomach, tilting her forehead toward him, beckoning him to follow her lead.

I rubbed my lips together, pressing them over my teeth as I pondered my cross-examination. Picking up my pen, I drew a vertical line down the center of a fresh page in my legal pad, preparing to take notes of his statements in one column and list the holes to poke through them in the other. I stared at the defendant when I was done.

Lawrence's lawyer repeated, "Whose gun was it?"

I crossed and recrossed my leg under the table, now bouncing my pen in my hand with anticipation.

"I don't know," he answered, lifting his chin, with an uncomfortable smile that quickly disappeared.

My eyes narrowed as I studied him.

"Lawrence?" said his lawyer, caught off guard. She twisted her head away from the jury. "Whose gun was in the car that day?" Her eyes flashed as she approached him. She sniffed and glanced at the jurors.

"I really don't know," he repeated.

My eyes drifted to the judge. He was staring back at me. I held his gaze. We both wanted an explanation.

"Why are you saying that you don't know?" she asked.

"Because all I know is that it wasn't mine." His eyes were looking past his attorney. We both followed his gaze to Trevor, who sat, seemingly stupefied by Babyface's words. "I don't know who it belonged to."

When I turned my head back toward the defendant, the judge audibly exhaled. He looked down and began typing, before leaning back, pouting, and then retracting his lower lip as he looked up at the ceiling.

I scanned the jury while the defendant's attorney gathered her thoughts. Several jurors were squinting at Babyface, incredulous. Others were looking at me with raised eyebrows. The juror who had been admonished for throwing up his hands during Trevor's confession no longer seemed annoyed with my decision to prosecute the defendant. Babyface's attorney began to walk backward toward the defendant's table.

She hovered around the table, flipping through her notes, searching. Stalling, perhaps, as she decided what to do next— whether to risk the defendant's further derailing the plan by asking the question on the tip of her tongue: *Why did you confess to it if it wasn't yours?* Instead she sat down, straightening her back as she covered her mouth, releasing it only to say, "No further questions."

I rose, confirming the statements in his confession without asking why he confessed to possessing a gun he now said was not his and without ever asking the question that was really on my mind: *Why didn't you save yourself when you had the chance?*

With every new response, his tone mimicked that of Trevor, emulating his sarcasm but without the wit. It was hard to decipher whether he was strategic or naive. His charm, once in abundance, now seemed unnatural and contrived. Sadly, I don't think it was. He may have just been trying to please the only person sitting in the courtroom that he seemed to care about: Trevor. His common sense succumbed to his need for acceptance.

The smiles that had endeared him to jurors just moments ago seemed repugnant now. The realization of his poor choice was contagious, infecting each juror with a sudden indifference to saving a person unwilling to save himself. Even if they thought he was innocent, they seemed to recoil from his refusal to say that he was. The jurors were no longer looking at him but rather at their laps, biding their time until he left the stand.

As he stepped down, he looked past me to Trevor, seeking affirmation. He kept his eyes fixed on Trevor as he walked back toward his table. Trevor tilted his head and left the courtroom. Babyface stared at the door, more worried by his abrupt departure than the look of wrath from his own attorney, a scorn that carried through her closing argument. She asked jurors to see the confession as that of an impressionable people pleaser and his refusal to admit the gun was Trevor's as the result of intimidation. The jury was unfazed by her appeal.

The courtroom was half-full as the jury filed back in from deliberations. Babyface's family, missing earlier, now joined those in the courtroom—to support him, seemingly in the belief that their presence would carry the day. I wondered if they would have made a difference had they come sooner. When the guilty verdict was read, Babyface's body was half turned toward the door, watching, waiting for it to open. His girlfriend cried while holding his mother's hand. His grandfather held the hand of his own daughter, the woman who had named her son Lawrence. She grunted with pain. Lawrence was still watching the door as the marshals handcuffed him behind his back.

"How old is he again?" the judge asked.

"Twenty-two," we said in staggered order, both of our voices trailing off with the realization of what that now meant for his future. We exchanged a knowing glance.

The judge's eyes flashed, suddenly enraged. "I've repeatedly asked this young man's age, counselor? You have repeatedly told me twenty-one. Have you misled the court?"

"His birthday was yesterday, Your Honor," his attorney said. The judge looked at me for confirmation. I scanned the file and nodded. I hadn't realized his birthday had been only yesterday. A familiar feeling of dread washed over me as I anticipated what was ahead for Babyface. I began to replay his testimony, trying to understand his choice.

He had gained another year of life but had lost his opportunity to still be classified as a youthful offender. There would be no program available to expunge his record now. His birthday disqualified him, graduating him into the world of adulthood accountability. He would carry a felony conviction for the rest of his life.

Meanwhile, Lawrence pled with his attorney, "Will you tell him where I am? Tell him what happened?" She shook her head, confounded by his fixation on Trevor.

"Forget him," she said. "I'll follow up with you."

We watched as he was led back to the cellblock, out of view. His mother's eyes stared at the cellblock door as she frantically asked his attorney what they were going to do to him and when she could see him. Could she just hug him before he went back? His attorney tried to calm her down and assure her that her son would be alright when the cellblock door opened again. An armed marshal walked out, holding something in his hand. He handed it to Babyface's attorney.

"What's that? Is it a note for me? What is it?" the mother begged.

"It's his belt, ma'am," she explained.

"Why? What? Why can't he have his belt? He wouldn't hurt anybody with it. It's for his pants. I don't understand."

Babyface's mother turned to me. "Why can't he have his belt?"

I looked at the judge and defense counsel for confirmation that I could answer. It came. "It's so he doesn't hurt himself, ma'am," I said quietly.

She screamed and collapsed into her husband's arms. I could still hear her screaming as I walked out of the courtroom, down the hall, with my closed file in hand. Trevor was in the hallway, making a young woman giggle as he leaned toward her against the wall.

His belt still on, he had not a care in the world.

8

There's Still Time

On Prosecuting a Mother for Child Abuse While
Faced with the Prospect of Losing My Own

My ob-gyn was calling.

I had a break from trial, so I stepped out into the hall to take the call.

"Hello? Gimme onnnne sec . . . ," I whispered, hurrying out of earshot of others in the loud hallway. I plugged one of my ears to hear more clearly.

"Hello?" I repeated.

"Hi, Laura! Did I catch you at a bad time?"

"Yes, kind of. I think I have a few minutes until I have to go back into the courtroom. I'm in trial today."

"Oh, we can talk later."

"No, no. I'm nervous now. Everything okay?" I giggled to comfort myself.

"Well, this will be quick. I just wanted to let you know that your tests came back. The fetus has an unexplained elevated alpha-fetoprotein level."

"What does that mean?" I froze. This was my first pregnancy, and I didn't yet have the perspective to weigh the information against my anxiety.

"An elevated alpha-fetoprotein level usually is an indication of spina bifida or some neural tube defect."

I clutched my stomach as I felt the tears welling in my eyes. I wasn't entirely sure what that was, but it didn't sound good. I waited for the doctor to elaborate. Nausea was overtaking my body, and I hesitated before swallowing to avoid the reflux.

"Don't worry," she said. My heart slowed and I started to exhale. "You're within the legal range to abort if you choose to do so. You don't have much time, but . . ."

"What did you just say?"

She repeated, ignorant of her upbeat tone. "You're still within the range to terminate your pregnancy. You want to call me after your trial? We can talk more then."

The nausea yielded to rage at the reflexive dismissal of my feelings and her unconscionable disregard for bedside manner. She was not my usual doctor but had been filling in while mine was away. "Do you have any idea how heartless that just was? Why would you tell me that news in that way?"

"Oh, I'm so sorry." She seemed genuinely stunned. "I didn't mean to offend you. I just knew you didn't have much time and you always seem so matter-of-fact. I'm really sorry about that."

"I seem so matter-of-fact so you thought it would be right to tell me not to worry because I could still abort my child?" My voice cracked as I clenched the phone.

A man walking by looked up as I spoke. I turned my head slightly, ducking it as if it would lower the volume of my voice. I visualized the path to my parking garage as I ground my teeth audibly. If I could just make it to my car, I would be alright, I thought. I leaned against the wall to keep from falling, scanning my mind for some memory of what spina bifida was. I had been unprepared for the word "abort," and I tried to shake it out of my mind. My husband and I had just chosen a name.

The court clerk scanned the hall, peering at me from the courtroom door I was staring at to keep from falling. She waved me back inside with a harried look. I seethed on the phone, suppressing fear and rage simultaneously.

"Are you able to come in this afternoon. I am just so sorry. I really didn't mean to deliver it that way. You don't have to terminate. I was just explaining . . ."

"Oh my God. Stop talking. Right now. Stop. I will be there this afternoon. I suggest you find someone other than you to meet with me. I want to talk to someone else—my actual doctor. About this. Today." I tried to calm my voice as the clerk called out my name, irritated.

I hung up the phone, shaking as I exhaled, denying my tears the chance to fall. I held on to the rage as I yanked back the heavy wooden door to the courtroom. My anger was the distraction I needed to keep from buckling. I had just one more witness, and if the defense didn't present a case, I could deliver my closing argument now. I calculated the time I had left and counted my blessings that this was only a bench trial to be decided by a judge, with no lengthy jury instructions to sit through. There would be no time to call my husband and let him know what was happening. I decided to wait.

The judge, a White woman, began heckling me the minute my foot appeared in the doorframe. "Thank you for gracing us with your presence again, government," she said, pointedly ignoring my agitation or oblivious to it. "Did you enjoy your phone call? Have a good chat? Maybe you were able to grab a latte?"

I didn't have the energy to fight her. No witty response awaited her. I looked down at my desk to collect my thoughts. She wasn't finished yet. "I told you I'd be right back to your case. Please don't disrespect the court's time again. You act like you have all the time in the world."

I remained silent. Funny, I was just told I hardly had any time left. "Your Honor, I didn't expect that call today. I apologize for disrespecting the court."

She studied my face. She hadn't expected my passivity. She looked at my torso, since I was still clutching my stomach.

"Is there something wrong with your stomach?" She leaned in. I wasn't visibly pregnant yet.

"No, Your Honor, there's nothing wrong," I said, trying to convince myself.

"Well then, call your next witness."

I did. I objected. I argued. I elicited the facts. And waited for the defense to present a case. They did. I objected and cross-examined. I desperately wanted to go on autopilot, detach emotionally, but the victim, a child physically abused by her own mother, deserved my full attention. She was somebody's daughter, even if her mother didn't deserve her. I inwardly winced each time I heard the word "child," letting it fuel my resolve and resentment that a mother could be so cruel to her child as I wanted nothing more than to keep mine.

I exhaled when I heard the verdict, not just because I had won but also because I was free to feel. I wasn't sure I wanted to. I grabbed my phone and called my husband as I tried to make it to the sidewalk outside. I couldn't catch my breath as the tears began.

"The doctor called."

"Where are you?" he asked, scared.

"I'm just leaving the courthouse now. I'm walking to the car."

"Stay where you are. I'm coming there now."

I made it as far as the appeals court across from the trial courthouse before I stumbled to the ground. I sat on the sidewalk crying, trying to gather the things that had fallen from my purse.

An older Black security guard in his fifties came running outside, holding his walkie-talkie.

"Oh my Lord. What happened? Are you hurt? Did somebody hurt you?" He pressed the talk button before reconsidering. "What happened, sweetheart? Did someone hurt you? Tell me what happened."

"No, nobody hurt me. I just . . . it's my baby. They said something might be wrong with my baby and I'm just trying to make it home, sir."

He looked at me with a fatherly gaze and helped me up. He hugged me as he lifted me to my feet. He sighed, unsure of what to say. "Can I call someone for you? I don't think you should be on the subway like this. Can someone drive you home?"

"I called my husband. He's coming."

My phone rang. It was my father. He always seemed to call when I needed him.

"Oh, Daddy," I cried.

My father's voice turned to concern. "Hel-hello? What's the problem? What is making you cry?" His phrasing always had a way of orienting you toward the cause of the emotion rather than the emotion itself.

I explained what had happened. The news. Her tone. The judge. The fall. The nice security guard who was standing beside me while we talked. That, yes, my husband, Dale, was on the way.

"Okay," he said, exhaling, signaling he had heard me and was prepared to respond. "You're gonna have to play the hand you're dealt. You always have and you always will. Sounds like you don't yet know what you've been dealt. You have to get more information. You know sometimes doctors make these statements for malpractice reasons. She did the wrong thing telling you that way. It was wrong, absolutely was. She made some assumptions about who you are, and what she thought you could take, and treated you that

127

way based on it. A mother can't hear something like that, delivered without regard for your feelings. I understand why you're upset. A father can't, either. And you *are* a mother now. And a lot of your decisions and your reactions will be driven by instinct. No one will teach you exactly what to do next. It'll be you. Somehow you'll know. And you're gonna have to learn to trust it. So, start asking yourself what your gut tells you. Do you feel like something is wrong with your baby?"

"No," I said. I realized I was still holding the guard's hand. I pulled it away and mouthed the word "sorry."

He held up his hands to say it was okay. And stood in front of me with eyes closed, head down, and hands woven together at his waist. He was praying.

My father said, "Well, there you go. Now, we don't know the deck yet. But you'll deal with whatever comes. And you'll figure it out. Spina bifida isn't a death sentence, but you'll have to under-stand if there's a quality-of-life issue. If there is, you'll do what's best for your family. Okay? Now, when will you have a chance to go to the doctor?"

"I'm waiting for Dale now—he's on his way to meet me and then I'll go there."

"Okay, call your mother. She may have something else to say that will help. She definitely will."

"Okay." I exhaled through protruding lips, like I was blowing a red-seeded dandelion.

My phone rang.

"I just got off the train. I'm walking to the courthouse," Dale explained. "Where are you?"

"I'll walk over to you. I'm just on the other side of the court-house. I'll head to you now."

I turned to the security guard. "Thank you, I'm okay now."

"Where are you walking? I'll make sure you get there."

"Just to the Metro. It's okay. My husband's walking this way now. Thank you, though. I'm sorry to have caused a scene like that."

"Nothing to be sorry about. My wife cried all the time when she was pregnant with our boy. I had to carry a box of tissues everywhere we went. Now he's getting ready to have a baby and she's cryin' about that." He tossed his hand and chuckled with the memory. "I'll walk you a little ways. Just till you see him. I wanna make sure you're alright."

"I see him now." I pointed to him and called his name. He turned toward the sound and searched for a moment. I repeated his name and he jogged toward us. "Thank you, really." I started to walk away, then turned around. "Congratulations on being a grandfather."

He smiled. "My third." He pointed his hand toward my husband. "Alright now," he said, passing me toward him.

"What happened? What did the doctor say?"

I explained, this time without tears. He sat down on a cement bench, leaning his head into my stomach as I stood. I repeated my father's words, adopting them as my own.

He nodded. "So what do we do now? Do you have an appointment already or are we supposed to just call?"

"No, I'm going there now."

"*We're* going there now. It's okay. It's going to be fine. It's just, we have to find out the information. It'll be okay."

He hugged me and kissed my hand once as we started to walk to the parking garage.

"Did you win?" he asked, trying to distract us both.

"What? Oh, my trial. Yes, yes, I won."

"Which case was this again?"

"The one where the mother told her she wished she were never born, the one with the burn marks." I always relayed the most disturbing details of a case in a shorthand way to people outside the prosecutors' office. Most people either couldn't emotionally process the details or they wanted you to reassure them, if not somehow guarantee, that the victim would be alright. Providing more information didn't help with either response. It also would force me to relive my own initial reaction to the case by seeing that of someone else. It was better for me to think of the completed trials simplistically to avoid churning the painful thoughts in my head.

"Geez. I forgot about that one," he recalled, not wanting me to elaborate further. "What kind of a mother would . . ."

I nodded my head in the direction of a pregnant woman with a baby in tow.

"That one," I said, pointing to the woman approaching the subway escalator. "There she goes now."

"I thought you won?"

"I did. But the judge gave her time served and hung time over her head. She's not going to jail today."

"That's not the girl with her now, is it?"

"No. She's with her father now. I think that little boy is her friend's son; he was with her in the courtroom."

"She's pregnant?" He stopped. "God bless that child."

"God bless ours," I said, holding back my tears.

For the next four months, I was plagued with anxiety about what might lie ahead for my child, but equally certain of my intent to fight for it and full of excitement and unconditional love for the baby that was growing within me. I approached my cases from the perspective of an unapologetically protective mother.

Each week, I left the courthouse, waving at the kind guard outside, to stare at indiscernible images on an ultrasound monitor while doctors tried to detect any possible birth defects, or any possible explanations for the abnormal test results. None ever came.

But my son did. He was born precisely on his due date, healthy and strong, with vocal cords to match.

The doctor confirmed that there were indeed no obvious signs of a neural tube defect before placing my crying son's head next to mine. He stopped crying and tried to focus his eyes on my face as I spoke my first words to my newborn son: "You were wanted." Because he was.

9

Not Their Son, Too

On Watching the Victim's Family Beg Not to
Have Their Son's Murderer Go to Prison

I still hear the wails.

These guttural cries traveled like a toxic gas across the courtroom, knocking each person over in the benches, causing their bodies to lean against one another in discombobulated comfort. Some stared ahead. Others leaned against those next to them, their necks pinned, unable to move or flee or succumb. It was a torturous scene, one that left you without recourse to process, a confusion of grief on both sides of the aisle.

Three families were in the courtroom: those of the two Black twenty-four-year-old defendants who were being sentenced for killing a man in a silly dispute over a woman they didn't even know, and the family of the twenty-four-year-old Black man they shot. None of the families could stomach the nearly lifetime sentences just doled out by the judge, sentences that likely would amount to an exponentially greater number of years than the ones the defendants had spent on this earth. The defendants panted as each added the number to their own age and realized the bullets they fired had just killed them too.

I had only entered the courtroom moments before. I had come

to handle a separate matter in that courtroom when I walked into the judge summarizing the case and explaining the sentences he had just handed down. My emotions were heightened, and hearing the wails brought tears to my own eyes as I tried to piece together the scene.

"Not their son, too!" the victim's mother cried out in horror. "Don't take him, too!" She choked on her words as she walked toward the mother of one of the defendants slumped in the aisle, wailing uncontrollably.

"Your Honor, please . . . not their son, too," the mother insisted, extending an outstretched arm toward one of the women. "My son is gone—don't take them, too. You're killing them, too!" She looked torn, unsure what to do with the hand at the end of her outstretched arm. It alternated from a finger pointed, to a hand half recoiled into a fist, to outstretched fingers extended in anguish.

"Please," the victim's father shouted. "Please, there's been enough loss already. We don't want this." His fist slamming on the front of the bench, his coat clenched in his hand as if he were about to leave. His coat lowered as his fist dropped.

"Son, we're here, son, we're here. We won't leave you . . . ," another man offered softly on the other side of the courtroom. "Look at me! Look at me!" Both defendants looked back, swallowing hard. I wondered which was his son.

The prosecutors remained standing, stoic in their attempt to keep their shoulders squared. One hung his head as he leaned forward on the table, balancing his weight on his fingers. The other placed her hands in her pockets, bouncing forward on her toes. They watched the judge. They had secured the conviction, but no one in the room seemed to equate it with justice.

Both defendants looked up toward the ceiling, glancing toward each other along the way. Each failed in his attempt to straighten his spine in an effort to appear strong. For one, the effort proved too much, and he went limp and fell to the ground.

A marshal rushed to his aid as he lay there. The judge leaned over, asking if a medic was needed. The marshal, a Black man in his thirties, raised his gloved hand and said, "He's fine, Your Honor. I've got this." As he helped the defendant to his feet, the defendant's middle-aged White attorney stepped aside and turned back to the public gallery, lifting his hands in distress. The marshal held on to the young man, leaning in toward him to whisper something in his ear. He then repositioned himself behind the defendant, shielding the back of his body from view.

Someone shouted, "Get away from him. You don't have him yet! I can't see him! Make him move!"

The marshal refused as the crowd grew more anxious, decrying his insensitivity and his failure to get medical assistance.

"He doesn't require medical assistance," the marshal stated flatly to the judge.

"They won't even get him a doctor—" a voice in the audience lamented. "They don't even care. He's just another nigga to them."

The Black marshal shook his head and flared his nostrils as he inhaled. He remained behind the defendant, shielding him from view.

The judge, an older Black man in his sixties, held up his gavel in mid-air and slammed it on the desk before him, hesitating as he considered whether to use it again. The gavel stood suspended, trembling at his wrist, as his mouth hung loosely, his eyes cast downward. His mouthed moved, but his words were not audible over the crowd's anguish.

"Order . . ." He tried to clear his throat. "I'll have order!" He held the gavel upright, like a post, pushing the base into the desk to brace his upper body as he rose. His body swayed subtly as he stood to face the public gallery, his fist tightening around the gavel.

With the gavel still upright in one hand, he slammed his free hand repeatedly on the desk. "I will have . . . order . . . in this courtroom," he growled, trying to display control. His eyes gave him away, though. He pushed his pursed lips out repeatedly as if trying to stiffen his lip and shield its tremble, running his tongue over the front of his teeth to release the saccharin film that appears when tears are imminent.

"Hear me . . . please," the judge said, almost ashamed.

The wailing was suppressed momentarily. Heads bobbed as everyone tried to focus on the prospect of mercy.

"What would you have me do?" the judge asked. "There are no winners here. One young man's life was taken, and justice must be served. I don't come to this decision lightly. I see another two young men before me who wish they could have made different decisions. Taken back that choice. To not have gotten into the dispute or shoot at anyone let alone into a crowd in what can only be described as a senseless act of violence. I bet you can't even remember the reasons you convinced yourself of at the time. I see two young men who will be older than me before they will have their first chance at parole, and will likely serve the rest of their lives in prison . . ."

"Please, Your Honor, please. Please, judge. Please," one defendant begged.

"I'm sorry, I'm so sorry. Please . . . ," he continued. "Tell him!" he cried, nudging his co-defendant as he turned his body to the crowd. "Tell him we're sorry! Tell him, please! Ma'am, I'm sorry, I'm so sorry. I didn't mean to kill your son. I'm so sorry. Please. Help me! I'm so sorry."

His knees buckled as he begged. His attorney helped him stay upright, holding his arm around his body for support.

The other defendant began to heave. The marshal remained behind him, creating distance between his body and the defendant's.

"Can they hug their families?" one defense counsel asked, already aware of the answer.

"No, there will be no contact for security reasons. Gentlemen"—the word "gentlemen" rattled around in my brain—"I have made my decision, taking into account the prosecutor's recommendation along with the sentencing guidelines, and I didn't make it lightly. Take note of all the people who were rooting for you. Even the family of the man you killed. Godspeed. Please step the defendants back."

I watched as the marshals led the young men out of the courtroom. They each looked back at their families reeling in anguish. The marshal continued to shadow the defendant who seemed particularly unsteady, shielding him partly from view by angling himself accordingly.

"Call the next case," the judge began, his throat clearing the tremble in his voice. The courtroom clerk pushed her glasses up as she discreetly wiped something from her face. She slowly dabbed a tissue under her nose to avoid drawing attention to herself. Her voice was feeble.

I waited before approaching the well of the courtroom, mistakenly believing that the judge intended for the public gallery to be cleared before we began. He hastened me instead, eager to conclude our case, which appeared to be his final matter of the day. I quickly rose, navigating around the family members still grieving as the sentence sunk in. My final obstacle was to pass the mother whose legs were buckling as she was escorted down the center aisle as if walking behind a coffin carrying her child.

Defense counsel and I moved to our respective tables, raising eyebrows toward each other as we simultaneously exchanged a head shake. White, in his forties, he looked toward the ground and raised his index finger toward his nose, as if he were trying to prevent a smell from seeping into his nasal passages. He clenched his eyes

137

for a moment and stood by the end of the table. I watched him as I announced my presence to the court.

"Laura Coates, on behalf of the United States, Your Honor," I said, gathering my thoughts as I opened my file before me. The smell of feces wafted toward me, drawing my attention to the desk where the defendants had been standing moments ago. The exchange between the marshal and the defendant who had fainted became clearer immediately.

The defendant had defecated on himself in fear. The marshal had been blocking this final humiliation from view. The marshal hadn't been indifferent or cruel. He protected this secret at the expense of being pilloried by the spectators in the gallery. He had stood behind him to hide the protrusion and the stain.

The marshal returned to approach the bench. The judge instructed the clerk to request disinfectant, before returning his attention to me. His expression was of a man obviously wounded but trying to focus on the welcome distraction of a comparatively trivial matter.

The judge and I were both robotic, aware of the weight of what had just happened and the cruelty of forward motion. The wheels of justice moved without regard to the emotional process.

"Ms. Coates, remind me of this case," the judge inquired. I squinted quizzically. The file was before him; the facts were not pertinent to the procedural objective.

"Please, government," the judge pleaded. "Indulge an old man today."

"Happy to, Your Honor. Although I'm not agreeing with the characterization of you as old," I offered, hoping to diffuse the tension with a moment of levity.

"I was young before today. Please go on," he responded, turning his attention to the file.

As I spoke, he alternated stroking his forehead with his ring and middle fingers. The middle finger would travel in one direction, his ring finger would retrace the other's path. He was withdrawn, until I invited his response: "Your Honor?"

He looked up, startled by the invitation, trying to reorient himself.

"You were going to set the next date on the calendar," the defense counsel offered.

"Yes . . . pulling up my calendar now . . . ," the judge said, returning to the moment for the duration of the brief hearing.

At the conclusion of the matter, the judge asked, "Is that all that's on the calendar this morning?" He sounded hopeful and exhausted.

"Yes, Your Honor," the clerk responded sympathetically. "I think that's enough for today, don't you?"

The judge nodded and stood. We stood as he left the bench.

"Don't stand for me today . . . not today," he said, waving his hand for us to carry on, not able to withstand being watched another moment.

As the defense counsel and I walked out of the courtroom, he asked if I had noticed the smell of feces. "That smell was just awful. I guess he shit himself, huh?" he said aloud, saddened by the reality, just as we crossed the threshold into the hallway to find the family members embracing one another in the hall. One of the mothers buried her sobs into the chest of a man humming into the top of her head.

"I gotta go. Call me later so we can discuss the plea, alright?" I said, walking away to put space between myself and the sorrow before me. He walked with me. Clearly he felt the need to discuss what we had just witnessed.

"Look, I gotta go," I repeated, pointing to my pregnant stomach and disappearing into the bathroom for a moment of peace. I hoped I wouldn't find him waiting outside, wanting to pick up where we left off—I wanted to forget what I had just seen in that courtroom. The sorrow was overwhelming. The victims' emphatic pleas for lenience had left me disoriented, and out of self-preservation I wanted to return to the state of mind I was in before I had heard the wails. I needed distance from the trauma.

Emerging from the stall, I found another woman washing her hands and face. I immediately recognized her as the mother who had shouted, "Not their son, too." I began lathering my hands as I looked into the mirror. Our eyes met.

"What are you having?" she asked, looking at a shirt spread thin across my round belly.

"I'm not sure yet," I said, not knowing whether to smile.

"Maybe a son . . ." She nodded, rinsing her hands under the water.

"Maybe," I said. Turning toward her. "I'm . . . I'm very sorry for your loss . . . I was inside the courtroom today. I'm very sorry," I stammered, trying not to offend, provoke, or patronize her.

She faced me, moving her lips between a wan smile and the formation of words. She nodded as she bit the inside corner of her lower lip, and inhaled to prevent her tears. You could hear the air somersaulting over the tears as she tried to hold them in.

"Can I?" she said, her wet hands outstretched toward my pregnant belly. I frowned with discomfort as I looked at her face. The sincerity of her emotion willed me not to recoil, and I nodded in assent. I moved my hands slightly away from my sides, allowing them to hover instinctively in my baby's defense.

She placed her hand on my stomach and closed her eyes for a moment, nodding heavily as if trapped in a memory. She stepped back, removing her hand as her tears overwhelmed the dam.

"Thank you," she said. "I bet it's a boy . . . you're gonna love that child . . . love being his mother."

"Yes," I said, smiling self-consciously, afraid to display an insensitive level of joy or optimism.

I instinctively placed my own hand where hers had been and realized that my shirt was wet. I made a face reflexively, which I instantly regretted, and softened my expression.

"Look at me," she said, rushing to grab a paper towel for my shirt. "I didn't even dry my hands . . . I've made your stomach wet. I'm so sorry."

"Oh it's okay, I don't mind. I didn't even notice, to tell you the truth." I smiled to reassure her, hoping the lie would help.

She used the paper towel for her hand, and then placed it on the door handle to leave. She paused for a moment, seeming to steel herself for the hallway. She looked back over her shoulder at me, nodding at my stomach in goodbye.

I lingered for a moment, feeling the wet handprint through my shirt as I straightened my coat, replacing my hair on the outside of the collar. I reached for a paper towel to dry the area, but stopped mid-stroke. Removing it felt oddly dismissive and cruel, an act of disgust—an emotion I certainly did not feel toward her.

I left the bathroom, expecting to pass her on my way down the hallway, or down the escalator, or outside the courthouse. But I never saw her. A part of me wanted to search. To pass by her again and give myself some reason to believe that perhaps she would be okay, someday. I knew she wouldn't be. And I knew that if I saw her again, I couldn't pretend she might be.

Out of the courthouse, the wind was unyielding and harsh. I started to button my coat as I walked briskly to my office. The wind was slicing my stomach at the damp handprint on my shirt, beckoning me to feel. I opened my coat so I could.

10

No One Who Had Been Raped Would Have

On Watching a Female Judge Victim-Blame
a Teenage Girl Based on Her Courtroom Attire

I saw her, too. Skipping down the center aisle, she was approaching the witness stand in an above-the-knee skirt, breasts bouncing unrestrained. She looked down, pulling her lips over her teeth to hide her smile. She peered out from the corner of her eyes, trying to see the spectators' reaction in her periphery.

Her hair was gathered in a bun atop her head, with an assortment of barrettes and clips fastening stray hairs in place. She giggled as she raised her right hand while she was being sworn in. She tugged at her skirt, lowering it closer to her knee. The skirt buckled along her hips, slightly twisting her zipper. Her body belied her age; she had a child's face on a woman's body. She stood fidgeting, uncertain of herself but quite accustomed to attention nonetheless. She straightened her spine, throwing back her shoulders and thrusting out her chest as she batted her eyes at the marshal.

He frowned, admonishing her with his disapproving glance. She slouched and tugged again at her skirt on one side. She finger-combed the back of her hair before rubbing the inner corner of her eye, flicking away what she had retrieved from the side of her face.

The girl remained standing, playing with her fingers as she looked toward the prosecutor waiting to be told what to do next. Her posture was awkward and uncomposed. She rubbed her glossed lips together and scratched under her nose as she waited to be told to sit down.

I had only entered the courtroom to handle a separate matter a few moments before she was called to testify. I was already exhausted. I was pregnant again, and my feet were swelling in my shoes. I discreetly took them off as I sat on the bench wiggling my toes and waiting for my case to be called during a break in this trial. She would be their final witness of the day. I knew the other prosecutors; they specialized in child sexual assault prosecutions this rotation. I could tell she was the victim by the way the defendant shifted in his seat when he saw her. He went rigid and folded his hands on the table in front of him, his face devoid of expression, no doubt trained by his defense attorney. Because she had not reported the assaults immediately, and he had continued to assault her over a period of time, the prosecutors had chosen to charge the assaults as misdemeanors to avoid a jury trial. A jury would be less likely to believe the victim, they assumed, because of the delayed report and the absence of physical evidentiary proof. Their hope was that the judge was better equipped to understand the psychology underlying the decision of a rape victim not to report the crime immediately and hopefully would preside over and decide a case without the baggage of preconceived notions about how a victim should or would behave.

But this judge had also noticed the victim. I instinctively shifted my gaze toward the judge as the girl giggled her way through the oath. The judge scanned the victim, furrowing her brow and turning the corners of her mouth down while she stroked her thumb under her chin before using it to crack each knuckle on her left hand. Her hand curled into a loose fist as she looked distastefully at the girl. She exchanged a glance with the marshal as he delivered the oath, prompting the admonishment his eyes relayed.

She cocked her head to the side as she looked the victim up and down, pausing periodically at each section of her body just long enough to convey her disgust. The girl waved at the prosecutor and lingered mid-air in the moment as she glanced toward the defendant before being told she could take a seat.

I couldn't reconcile the judge's expression with objectivity or even an open mind. I recognized it instantly as premature judgment. The kind of judgment one would expect from a first-time juror with a preconceived notion of what kind of person was entitled to be considered a victim; a preconceived notion of how they would act, dress, speak, process, or grieve. The kind of judgment that bench trials were supposed to prevent by virtue of a judge's rejection of those false assumptions. But there it was, judgment as evident as the immaturity of the child on the stand, brazen as the judge's disinterest in hearing a word from the victim.

Without knowing a single fact of the case, or the strength of the evidence against the defendant, I knew my colleagues had lost their case. The judge's focused glare on the child's appearance said everything. The defendant would be acquitted after the government rested. I saw that the defense counsel knew it too, by the sly smirk that briefly contorted his face to one side.

I waited, watching her testimony unfold, if only to see whether my prediction was right. I wanted to be wrong. I debated internally, willing myself to believe that I had misread her expressions, that I was merely projecting my own assumptions of how a juror would feel onto the enrobed judge.

Swallowing between sentences, the victim described rape at the hands of the man she called her father. He wasn't her biological

LAURA COATES

father, but he had been with her mother for years and had practically raised her since she was a toddler. A few years ago, they had moved in together, and she had her own bedroom for the first time. He had helped her paint it, in her favorite colors, she noted, pointing to the barrettes in her hair and a beaded charm bracelet on her wrist in the same palette as additional proof. Her mother had not been working recently, because she had health problems that made it hard for her to stand for long periods of time. Her father had been paying all the bills and had a habit of reminding them of it when her mother protested anything. Her mother wanted to get married, and he cruelly dangled the prospect of marriage as leverage, mocking her every chance he got.

The assaults began when the victim was still prepubescent, intentionally to avoid pregnancy, just as her mother's unexplained illness "made her start sleeping a lot."

"Your mother used to look good. Now look at her," he would say to her and the other children, forcing them to join him in shaming her for her appearance. "She doesn't keep herself up. Always sleeping. Can't do anything else but sleep, sitting around eatin' off me."

Her mother would often try to stand and put herself together, even setting an alarm before he came home, but she always fell short of his expectations. His attention turned to her daughter. As her body changed and developed, the nature of his attention did as well. What began as over-the-clothing massages and gyrations along her pubic area as he held her in a prolonged hug quickly shifted to forced oral sex and penetration.

The assaults were accompanied by emotional abuse. He called her ugly and undesirable, and this was followed by manipulation that often pitted her against her mother, who was aware of the assaults. The girl described how this abuse had destroyed her relationship with her mother, who vacillated between calling her a liar and

22.

blaming her for enticing her boyfriend out of spite and contempt. Her mother was eager to believe that her daughter was merely misinterpreting benign attention and misconstruing it as sexual. Her man would never do something like that, but her daughter, she somehow believed, would.

It was difficult to hear and nearly impossible to stomach. I questioned how this girl would fare later, in her adult relationships, with the memory of this moment, the trauma of the assaults at the hands of her father, the emotional abandonment of her mother, and the undeserved shame she might herself impose and carry.

She nervously giggled as she described how he touched her—she was unable to decide how to hold her hands and arms. She crossed her arms, clasped her hands, sat on them, with each movement becoming more self-conscious, fidgeting and apologizing for it with an insecure laugh, explaining her tendency to do that when she was nervous.

"Why are you giggling?" the prosecutor asked, already aware of the answer.

"I'm sorry. I'm just really nervous. I'm sorry. It's not that I think anything is funny. I'm sorry. I just, I'm just not sure how to . . . how to be." She exhaled and straightened her back, hoping her posture would convey her intentions. She looked down, noticing her breasts, and slouched to make them less apparent. She pulled her shirt collar to prevent the fabric from clinging to her skin, trying in vain to stretch her jean vest to cover her chest, but it was too small. She crossed her arms over her breasts to cover their appearance.

"I'm sorry," she repeated. She smiled sheepishly in submission and her eyes darted around the courtroom before settling on her mother. Her expression suggested that her last "sorry" had been for her. I turned my head to steal a glance at her mother. Her purse was in her lap, the strap wrapped around her hands like brass knuckles.

147

She was looking straight ahead, her eyes never meeting her daughter's. Instead she seemed to be staring at the water pitcher next to the defendant. Her breathing was trained, but her shoulders shook at the end of each exhale.

The daughter continued her testimony, speaking about how her mother's boyfriend would get jealous when boys her own age gave her attention. Then she described the attention, at times affectionate, at times violent, he would bestow upon her as a result.

"Why did you keep going along with it?" the prosecutor asked.

The question made me grimace. It implied she had somehow consented to the disgusting acts, like a passenger on a joyride.

"He said I wasn't ugly anymore when I did it."

The words hung in the air like a deep fog, tormenting the audience with the realization of the depth of his manipulation and its profound effect on her feelings of self-worth. She finger-combed the back of her hair again, her charm bracelet chiming as her hands moved. There was a unicorn dangling from the elastic rope. I wiped the tear that had escaped from under my glasses.

"But why didn't you tell anyone what was happening?"

"My mother already knew. That's why she hates me so much."

Again, I looked at the mother. She had lowered her eyes, which were now fixed on the defendant's left hand, which was subtly pressing against the table in front of him. There was something contorted, strained about the way he did this, as if he were stretching his wrist. His palm was vertical, his fingers were folded, his thumb underneath the table. It forced his arm to straighten, drawing his left shoulder downward. That's when I noticed his wedding band. And hers. Apparently he was no longer just the boyfriend, and that reminder served to suppress the mother's reaction to her daughter's accusation that she knew he had been raping her own child. After a beat, he folded both hands in front of him. His elbows now rested on the armrests of the chair he sat in. The mother's gaze remained where his hand had been. She violently wiped a tear hanging from her jaw before it gave her away.

"Did you tell anyone else?"

"My brother did. That's how come the police came."

"How did he know? Did you tell him?"

"He saw us once. Saw what I was doing to him."

I held my cheek with my hand, pushing the frame of my glasses off my face as she relayed the experience.

"And what is your relationship like with your family now—with your mother, I mean?"

"They don't like me." With that she began to cry, and a choreographed routine of courtroom staff prepared for such an event ensued. A box of tissues would be handed to the bailiff, who would then hand it to the witness, as the court reporter rested her hands for a moment, unable to transcribe that which was inaudible. The prosecutor would assure her that it would be okay and to take her time, suppressing the urge to fill the air to lessen the discomfort. The discomfort was the point. The judge would use the time to evaluate the sincerity of the victim's tears.

I studied the judge as she watched the girl cry. She squinted, and her jaw lowered slightly as she pressed her chin back toward her neck, trying to conceal a yawn. Her nostrils flared as she pressed her lips together to prevent the yawn's escape. Her fist concealed the rest as she turned away from the girl and began to type on the keyboard, now fixated on watching the words fly across her monitor. She raised her eyebrows as she typed, as if writing something that was bemusing to her. I wondered what aspect of the girl's painful testimony could possibly be eliciting her expression. Periodically she paused to look the victim up and down, at one point leaning toward the witness box over the edge to remind herself of the girl's appearance. The girl noticed her stares and replaced her crossed arms over her chest. The judge typed again, but this time with an air of indignation, at one juncture even silently, briefly throwing her head back in a smirk. The girl continued to cry.

Meanwhile, the courtroom benches had transformed into church pews as hushed whispers of ridicule and judgment of the defendant rose like hymns. Others in the public gallery began to murmur, a few of them quickly silencing themselves after they'd released an audible indication of disgust, their eyes darting back to the defendant as they shook their heads in derision. With each new recollection of rape, the victim's credibility increased, becoming progressively more detailed, more vivid, more disturbing as the memories marched toward the present. Vague date ranges of assaults turned into specified dates that she connected to family events, church events, basketball games, school pictures, her mother's birthday.

"And that's her mother right there sitting behind him like that," I heard one woman say through sucked teeth, while others shifted uncomfortably in their seats.

"And she knew?" another offered, incredulously.

The defendant sat stoically, as counseled by his attorney. Exasperated sighs peppered the courtroom as heads swiveled to exchange shocked and disgusted glances. But my eyes never left the judge. She was unfazed by the murmur, unaffected by the tears, her face frozen in the same dismissive expression of a person waiting for a tantrum to end.

"Please continue your questioning, government," the judge interjected as the girl's wails quieted. The prosecutor continued briefly, ending with a question about the girl's inability to sleep. Now, it was time for the defendant's attorney to steer the conversation.

Placing her elbow on her chair, the judge pressed her cheek into her palm and looked out at the gallery, scanning the faces that were trained on the witness. She swiveled side to side in her chair, sliding her palm from her cheek to cover her lips and exhale over the web between her thumb and index finger. Our eyes met as she rested her head back on the chair and placed her tongue on her top front teeth. She held my gaze for a moment, the base of her tongue exposed as the testimony restarted. Without lifting her head from the chair, she turned her head back toward the witness with a laborious blink, remaining in that position until the defense counsel rose for cross-examination.

I watched as he attacked the girl's memory, motives, and honesty with the indelicacy of an interrogator who knew he didn't have to be mindful of a panel of jurors expecting kid gloves to be used with a young victim. The judge would be unreceptive to the antics of showmanship that failed to move the needle, and he knew it. But it didn't mean he wouldn't try to toe the line. The judge met and resolved objections with the vigor of a sloth. She only came to life when the victim paused to cry, at which point she would lift her head from her chair and start tapping away on her keyboard, punctuating the end of each sentence with an exaggerated keystroke.

When questioning resumed, she leaned forward against her crossed arms resting on the desk and looked up at the clock on the back wall for the duration. Her arched eyebrow was the only indication she was even awake.

"You can get up," the judge said at the end of questioning. Just as before, the girl stood in the witness box, waiting for instructions on what to do next. She tugged at her skirt, trying to yank it toward her knees. She nervously scraped the back of her hair, pushing up any errant strands back toward her bun, this time snapping a barrette back in place.

"Do I go back to my seat now, Judge?" she asked meekly.

"Mmm-mmm. Yes. You can step down," she mumbled. As the

victim stepped down, I followed the judge's eyes as she watched the girl continue to tug at her skirt unsuccessfully. But I also noticed how the girl's gait changed as she neared the defendant, and how she veered toward the prosecutor's table in avoidance.

Before the prosecutor spoke, the judge announced that they would pause this trial, call a different case, and briefly address a scheduling issue in that matter. Realizing it was my case that would be called, I quickly scrambled to put my shoes back on, lamenting my decision to remove them in the first place. Without the confines of the shoes, the swelling had increased, making it difficult for me to insert my feet painlessly. I gathered my file, leaving my bag on the bench, and prepared to stand. I was twisting my foot, trying to wrench my heel into the back of the shoe, as the girl made her way through the swinging half door separating the well of the courtroom from the audience. She had yet to sit down when the judge told the clerk to call the next case. The girl paused in the bench in front of me, swiveling around to hear the judge, mistakenly thinking that the judge was speaking to her for a moment. Up close, the girl's youth was even more apparent. Her eyes had swollen from the tears, giving her the appearance of a child waking up from a nap. She looked back at me, unsure whether to hold my gaze. She swallowed as she anticipated judgment, her eyebrows lifted at the center expectantly, like a child waiting for scorn.

I blinked once conspicuously and smiled thinly as I nodded to reassure her. Her bottom lip trembled, making small indentations in her chin. I held my smile as I watched her turn to look at her mother, who continued to stare aimlessly ahead, frozen. There was more than one victim in the room.

I managed to squeeze my swollen foot back into my shoe as my case was being called. Approaching the portable wooden lectern that had been slid to the edge of the prosecutors' table, I held up my hand to my colleague as she tried needlessly to move her files out of the way to make room for me.

"Oh, it's okay." I reassured her, waving her hand away, knowing that my time before this judge would be brief before her trial would resume.

She asked what I thought of the girl's testimony by raising her eyebrows. I closed my eyes quickly and nodded subtly with my lower lip pouted to reassure her. I knew she had failed, but it wasn't because of anything she did wrong. There was no need to add to the anxiety.

After a brief admonishment from the court for the parties not to go far, the defendant, the girl's mother, and their lawyer retreated from the courtroom as the girl was ushered separately to a nearby room to wait.

I stood up, momentarily swapping with my colleague at counsel table for the duration of the short status hearing. My own trial before this judge would start within the next week, and this would be our final scheduling conference. My matter was by no means urgent, and although I found it odd that she would interrupt a trial to address it, it was quite common for judges to pause bench trials to address other brief matters on their docket. I studied the judge, hoping to decode if her tone would switch with cases. But she displayed the same indifference and haughtiness, and for a moment I hoped that I had misinterpreted her facial expressions earlier. Perhaps she wasn't judging the girl in the manner I thought after all. Somehow, however, I knew she didn't deserve the benefit of the doubt, and my gut couldn't convince my mind to be optimistic.

Between statements, the judge looked at the clock like she had somewhere else to be, occasionally turning her head laboriously from her computer to me as if it were a weight her neck couldn't support. The defense counsel asked to approach on a private matter.

She agreed by pushing the white noise button beckoning us to her sidebar.

We staked our positions, standing shoulder length apart, softly speaking in the court's direction. The judge started to lean in closely and moved her coffee cup out of the way, grabbing it by the mouth to place it on the other side of her monitor, angling the monitor slightly to make room for the cup. The angle revealed what was now on her screen: a shoe-shopping website. While a child had poured her heart out relaying the trauma of serial rape without the benefit of even her mother as either a protector or champion, the judge was trying to find a cognac knee-high boot that fit an extra-wide calf. I wondered what exactly she had been typing during the girl's testimony. I quickly scanned the tabs on the bottom of her screen to see if a Word document had even been opened. I touched my forehead and slid my hand down along my cheek, letting the cold tip of my pinky rest on my eyelid. The callousness was beyond what I had expected, and in that moment my suspicions of an acquittal were confirmed. She hadn't even had the decency to minimize the page as we approached. I tried to focus on what she was saying without narrowing my eyes in obvious anger, a task that proved so herculean that I lowered my head as if pondering the defense counsel's statements just to avoid having to behold the cynicism of a woman who held a young girl's fate in her hands. I doubted her ability to prioritize the well-being of a child when she had the attention span of one so eager to return to her own vapid pursuits. I made a mental note to tell the prosecutors after trial. There wasn't anything that could be done in the moment.

The defense counsel concluded his need for banter at the bench, and we returned to the silence of a courtroom unhushed by white noise.

The judge confirmed the trial date on the record and reminded the parties of briefing deadlines. She yawned before she sipped from her mug and returned to scrolling, undoubtedly procuring the priorities in her cart. She yawned again, blinking her eyes and smacking her tongue before asking the clerk to restart the trial. Before doing so, the clerk alerted me that another judge wanted me to immediately return to a different courtroom to handle another case.

"Can I tell them you're coming now?" the clerk asked.

"Yes, thank you," I replied. My preference to remain here and watch the remainder of the trial was irrelevant.

"If you see the parties, can you send them back in, please?" the clerk asked me. She was shuffling through paperwork and hoped to avoid having to get out of her seat.

"No problem," I said, turning toward the exit.

I hurried out of the courtroom, suspecting I knew where they would be. I knocked on the closed door to a private room nestled between two sets of double doors, adjacent to the courtroom. I relayed the message as my colleague opened the door. She had been speaking with the girl inside. She thanked me, starting immediately to the door.

"I have to go back in," she said over her shoulder before pausing. "You did nothing wrong."

The girl sat awkwardly in the room, tears running down her face as she tried to catch her breath. She accepted a tissue from an outstretched hand. As the door closed, I saw an arm wrapping around her shoulders to catch her falling head.

My heart sank for her. The arm didn't belong to her mother but a relative stranger who had become her champion and victim advocate. I wondered what it was like for her to receive compassion from a stranger while still trying to process rejection from her mother. I touched my stomach and made a silent vow to my child as I watched the heart of someone else's child break.

I tried to race upstairs to the courtroom, laboring under the weight of a pregnant belly as I climbed the escalator stairs. I gripped the railing and rode the last few seconds, trying to catch my breath so I wouldn't appear flustered when I reached the judge. I had to hurry. Judges were as notorious for their impatience as they were inconsiderate of anyone else's time. I didn't want my scheduling window to close in the courtroom—it would force me to return later in the day. I stood outside the courtroom with a distracted mind. I wondered whether the girl would watch the closing arguments that I was now missing. Would she react to the inadvertently callous summations of her trauma? Would her mother acknowledge her in any way or continue to stare blankly ahead, emotionally detached and cruelly defeated? Would my prediction of an acquittal come true?

These thoughts would have to wait. As I entered the courtroom, the clerk immediately called the case before I had even approached the rail. She added apologetically, "Government, I'll need you to stand in for a few other matters as well . . ." and motioned toward the paperwork on the desk.

I buried my thoughts and refocused on the matters before me, quelling my curiosity and impatience by estimating how long each side's closing arguments would be. I wanted to be there for the verdict, which, in a bench trial, was often immediately announced without a recess for deliberation. I still hoped that I had misread the judge's demeanor or perhaps that her lack of focus on the girl's testimony was because she had already heard enough to convict. In any event, I wanted to hear her reasons for her ultimate verdict and the courtroom's reaction to it. Judging from the minimal volume of paperwork and the judge's impatience in resolving my assigned matter, I surmised I'd have just enough time to make it back if this judge moved at even a moderate pace.

"Would you like to sit for these hearings?" the judge asked, looking at my stomach. "I give everyone the choice if you have a preference."

"No, but thank you, Your Honor." I was reluctant to sit, afraid it would invite the judge to be leisurely in his approach. I needed to see the ruling.

"Very well," he said. "You just let me know if you change your mind. No need to ask."

"Thank you, Your Honor. I might just take you up on the offer in a little bit," I said, wanting to convey my gratitude for the consideration. He smiled, pleased with himself for having made the offer.

"I've been here before," he said, trailing off with a "suit yourself" kind of tone.

After about forty minutes, I found myself wondering if he were belaboring matters just to prove himself right. Even the clerk was beginning to show her impatience. The slow pace didn't fit the court's perfunctory roles in these matters.

I relented, hoping that he was merely, and perhaps subconsciously, trying to prove that his chivalry was not misguided.

"I think you were right, Your Honor," I said, consciously coquettish. "I think I do need to sit if we go on much longer. I hope the offer still stands."

"Of course," he said, shaking his head and lifting his hands upward in response to sage advice finally heeded.

It had the intended effect. We dispensed with the next three matters in the time it took to complete the first. I thanked him for the consideration.

"I'd have offered it to anybody." He puffed his chest while attempting to deflate any argument that his grace was gender-specific.

I walked quickly through the hallways, stuffing files into my bag. The smells of the courthouse were making me feel ill, and I unwrapped a piece of gum to stave off nausea as I slipped back into the courtroom. I chewed precisely, careful not to breathe in the odors through my mouth.

The defense counsel was just wrapping up his final remarks as the door closed behind me. The prosecutors waived their rebuttal.

The judge cleared her throat and leaned in, readying herself for the pounce. She wasted no time on reflection and revealed the notes she had apparently been taking during the testimony, painstakingly recounting the details of the statements to which she assigned truth.

"I credit the fact that the defendant is her mother's boyfriend . . . I credit that he displays qualities of an emotional abuser toward herself and her mother . . . I credit that she is in fact a minor and the defendant is an adult and that the stepfather/stepdaughter dynamic does indeed qualify as a significant relationship under the law . . . I do not, however, credit the witness's statements regarding the allegations of sexual impropriety or assault." Her last line landed with a thud.

"Where is the witness?" she asked, which even a cursory inspection of the room would have revealed. She wasn't ignorant of her location; she was putting the victim on notice that the next part was meant for her.

Her arched eyebrow immediately revealed the acquittal as she unleashed on the victim's testimony. The judge didn't mince words about the victim's appearance and its effect on her judgment. I cringed at the mere thought of the impending persecution.

". . . No one who has been raped, even a young teenager, would have skipped down the aisle of the courtroom dressed like that. I don't know who dressed her, but her clothes were ill-fitting, and she was not even wearing the appropriate undergarments, not even tights. The skirt was barely covering her behind, and she didn't seem to mind. She giggled through her testimony not like a child assaulted but like one who thought there was something funny about wasting the court's time . . ."

This coming from a woman who preferred to spend the trial shopping.

From the moment I heard the words "no one who has been raped would . . . ," I turned to look at the victim. She stared at her bare legs, looking confused. She touched her hair, scraping the fallen hairs back up from the nape. I saw now it was a part of a nervous tick. The longer the attack on her appearance went on, the more she bit her nails, self-conscious and visibly distraught as she looked at her mother across the aisle. Her mother, though, never turned toward her, adhering to her trancelike state, this time nodding incessantly as if processing the moment rather than in assent.

"Cuz of how I look?" I heard the girl ask her de facto champion sitting next to her. The woman shushed her—she was trying to hear the absurdity of the judge's ruling in its entirety.

". . . sitting here cross-armed with an attitude as she suddenly recalled dates with the apparent aid of the prosecution."

A grunt escaped my lips as I sat stunned, hearing the way the judge used the victim's decision to shield her breasts under crossed arms against her. The judge looked up and paused, lifting her eyebrows as a belligerent dare for me to make another sound. I lowered my chin and lifted my eyes. I knew I had no recourse but wondered whether my colleagues who were actually trying the case would respond.

Sitting back in their chairs, the prosecutors were incredulous, enraged not only by the verdict but by the outsized and grossly inappropriate emphasis the judge had placed on how a testifying witness was dressed at trial. Not only was it irrelevant, but it disregarded the fact that she had been abused over the course of years in a variety of settings under a variety of circumstances, which had been described with specificity, the aftermath of which was corroborated. But whether her abuser would be held accountable ultimately came down to one person's assessment of how she expected a victim to act in that moment. The judge exhibited a total and complete disregard for the ills of victim-shaming. The assumption of a judge's objective empathy had proven to be a fatal miscalculation, and I wondered if a jury would have reacted differently.

Unlike for a defendant who is found guilty, there is no meaningful opportunity for appeal when a prosecutor loses their case. Double jeopardy had just attached, and you cannot have two bites at the apple in the form of a do-over. One of the prosecutors looked back at the girl, who stared back at them. That same prosecutor then closed her eyes while simultaneously rubbing her sinus with pinched fingers and gesturing with her other hand for the victim to wait for her to explain what had just happened, and why. I wondered how she would explain it; I bet she did, too.

Observing this interaction, I hung my head, not in anger but in sorrow, unable to watch this child try to understand what about herself had warranted such contempt.

The judge banged the gavel for effect and rose to strut through her escape tunnel that was her private door. The courtroom rose, as was customary, but I couldn't bring myself to stand under the facade of reverence. From my seat, I watched as a girl followed the crowd, tugging her skirt along the way, now painfully aware of just what the judge thought of her. She looked again at her mother, who had managed to stand up for something, just not for her.

As the judge's private door closed, the defendant rose with excitement, pumping his fists by his waist. He turned to hug the victim's mother.

"Time to go home, beautiful," he said, kissing her.

The victim stood watching the back of the prosecutors' heads, staring ahead as her mother had while she grieved convulsively on the stand.

She had nowhere else to go.

11

She's Always Been
Such a Good Girl

On Cross-Examining a Naive and Helpless
Mother Trying to Defend Her Daughter on Trial

My unborn baby kept kicking me. Through the jury selection. Through the opening statement. Through the direct examinations. Through the expert testimony. Through the photographs of the assault. Through the medical testimony.

Two mothers were on trial for savagely assaulting a pregnant woman in an unsuccessful attempt to kill her unborn child. One defendant, Kim, was the scorned ex-girlfriend; the victim, her replacement. The other was the ex-girlfriend's cousin.

And here I was, standing through swollen ankles with my own unborn baby thrashing within me as the victim compared the size of her pregnant belly at the time of the assault to my own now. I was slightly further along in my own pregnancy than she had been in hers at the time, but she was saying that she'd had the same unmistakable stomach of an obviously pregnant woman.

"Is there any way someone would not have known that you were pregnant? Were you showing?" I asked.

"I was really big. Anybody could tell I was pregnant. I was the same size as you. My stomach looked like yours." My daughter

161

kicked and I wondered what effect the defendants' blows would have on a baby capable of delivering kicks with such force. Surely she would have been capable of feeling pain. The jury stared at my stomach, no doubt wondering the same thing.

The defense attorneys objected in unison to the comparison to my stomach. We approached as a group, each of us vying to be the one facing the jury so we could manipulate our expressions to convey that we had the upper hand, irrespective of the judge's ruling.

Pregnant, I wasn't as quick on my feet as my colleagues and was the last to reach the judge's bench. My back was to the jury.

The more bombastic defense lawyer angled his body toward the jury as he whined his complaint with a mismatched expression of confidence. "Your Honor, the prosecutor is trying to prejudice the jury by using her own stomach as evidence."

I held out my hands to my side. "Your Honor, what would you have me do? I made no mention of myself. She answered an open-ended, non-leading question. I can't help the obvious comparison."

"Overruled. What would you possibly have her do?" She turned to me. "Be careful not to cross a line, though, Ms. Coates. I know, I know. But it must be said."

"Of course, Your Honor. But just to avoid having to do this every time she mentions her baby, let me also assure you that I'm not telling my own baby to kick nonstop." I turned to the bombastic one mockingly. "I just want you to know I'm really pregnant and it's not a pillow on a timer."

She kicked on cue.

The other attorney stifled a laugh and the judge sent us packing, but not before the bombastic one exclaimed, "Thank you, Your Honor, I appreciate it," while looking at the jury.

She continued to kick when the evidence obliterated their alibis and pinpointed their location. She kicked when the judge sustained objections. She kicked when they were overruled.

She visibly shifted beneath my suit jacket, forcing me to adjust the fabric, as I asked permission to approach the defense's final witness for cross-examination. The witness was not unbiased. She was the mother of one of the defendants, indeed the only one called (and perhaps willing) to testify in defense of either of the women. Her daughter, Tina, was not the ringleader but the tagalong who had joined in on the assault. She wasn't there to defend both women. Tina's mother's goal was singular: to protect her own daughter. Both women were being tried together, but the jury was not required to render the same verdict for the two. She hoped her testimony would lead at least to her daughter's acquittal, if not her niece's.

The mother smiled with her lips pressed together as I approached her, unsure of what lay ahead. I mirrored her smile as I began.

Cross-examination is tricky. You never ask a question you don't already know the answer to. In fact, you hardly ask any questions. The point is to elicit the equivalent of an affirming nod as you lead the witness through your own testimony, confirming aspects of your case that you need to incorporate during your closing argument. The overt "gotcha" is rare, not because it's impossible to achieve but because it's a bad strategy. Broadcasting the defendant's evidentiary shortcomings invites corrections, sudden calculated recollections, and sympathetic explanations that could fatally undermine your case. With surgical precision, you must extract only that information that buttresses your case, without alienating the jury by berating the witness. With a mother, the task is exponentially more delicate.

A mother is the most sincere witness but the least credible. Her loyalty is clear, and it does not lie with the person prosecuting her child. She wants to be helpful, and the jury empathizes with her plight. An oath becomes a suggestion to be forthcoming, not a mandate to be forthright. She will tell her truth, just not *the* truth. And you can't attack a mother trying to protect her child without forfeiting your own goodwill in front of the jury.

With delicacy in mind, I approached this mother, with my own soon-to-be daughter competing for my attention. She had been called for the sole purpose of being a character witness for her daughter alone, testifying only to her glowing and redeeming qualities. But the bombastic lawyer had gotten too cocky, which had made him careless. Tina's mother hadn't been in the courtroom to hear her daughter's testimony, and the lawyer had accidentally elicited an answer from her that fatally contradicted that testimony. I wondered if he had been listening to his client as she testified, and why he even chose to call her as a witness. Her testimony had only hurt her daughter's case. He had failed to realize his mistake and had continued with his questioning, eliciting additional contradictions.

The other attorney did realize the mistake and looked my way to see if I'd caught it. My co-counsel, added to the team in case I went into labor during trial, also noticed. She began frantically writing a note with such fervor that she shook the table. She tapped the note as she passed it to me. I was aware that the jurors had noticed her physical reaction. I discreetly waved my hand in her direction, sliding it horizontally in the air as it hovered over the table, an attempt to remind her to remain composed. I was not a prosecutor who broadcast her emotions gratuitously. The goal was not to be stoic but strategic. Jurors are unpredictable, and you don't have the luxury of being presumptuous about how they will interpret your reaction. Not only could reacting gleefully to the misstep of a testifying mother turn a jury against us, but my own moral compass rejected it wholeheartedly. As a mother myself, I felt sorry for her in that moment. She had tried and failed to help her daughter. I knew that I would now be able to capitalize on the contradictory testimony and confirm that her daughter was not with her at the time of the assault. After a beat, I glanced at my colleague's note: "HE JUST OPENED THE DOOR—WE GOT 'EM." All caps, underlined twice.

I touched the note to show I had seen it and laid a thumbs-up against the table. I held my hand on top of it to stop her from writing more. She sat back, now satisfied we were on the same page. I wondered if she had misinterpreted my composure as dazed.

Here I was, standing before a mother afraid for her daughter but oblivious to the damage her own testimony had just done. My questions would be brief, not providing time for her to either correct or lament. I only needed the mother to confirm that she couldn't corroborate her daughter's alibi. But I would approach it indirectly.

Poking a hole in someone's alibi is par for the course for any prosecutor. But today felt different. A sadness came over me about what lay ahead. I dreaded having to use a mother as a vehicle in her daughter's prosecution. I felt angry with the defense attorney for making her take the stand. The evidence against the defendants was already overwhelming. Surely he couldn't have reasonably believed that her testimony would move the needle.

But watching the way she looked at her daughter, I knew she could not have been convinced to sit idly by and leave it up to fate. I also knew I would have made the same choice to help however I could.

"Ma'am. You obviously love your daughter, Tina. Any mother would . . ."

She nodded. "I do. She's always been such a good girl." A mother will never address a character flaw. She will only view it as an aberration and dismiss any need for accountability.

"And you are a good mother," I said emphatically, careful not to convey even the slightest hint of sarcasm or condescension. Her parenting was admittedly irrelevant. Her daughter, Tina, was a grown woman with four children of her own, but I assumed she felt judged by me, and I didn't want her to feel attacked. "You've raised her well, I know . . . teaching her right from wrong and instilling good values along the way . . . any loving mother would . . ."

Hearing those words aloud sobered me, and I thought of the mother victimized by these defendants, choosing to clutch her pregnant stomach instead of shielding her face or head. My allegiance lay with her, reminding me to prioritize my empathy. I compartmentalized my emotion from my directive to avoid being consumed with guilt.

"I raised my children with the Lord."

"Oh, I know you are a woman of faith . . ." I smiled warmly. She returned my smile, lifting her head with pride. A woman in the jury nodded an affirming smile. I remembered the juror's reference to her faith during voir dire.

"Is your church close to your home—you live right near that diner near the corner of—"

"Yes." She replied before I had completed my question, to be helpful.

She lived near the corner where the assault had happened. Her daughter's cell phone had been pinpointed to that location, at that time, a fact the defense had argued was not incriminating but indicative of the fact that she was with her mother, at her home, in the middle of a workday.

"And is it Grandma or Nana . . . what do those grandbabies call you?"

She smiled, "I'm Grandma or 'Momma number two.'" She giggled toward her daughter. "Momma number one."

"I bet they love going to Grandma's house . . . and you stuff them and return them all sugared up." I laughed reservedly as she affirmed.

"I do. I keep them sometimes at night when she goes to school. She's working very hard on herself, always been a good student. But I work during the day, so I do what I can at night to help her."

"You make them dinner?"

"Oh, they love Grandma's food. My daughter is getting better at cooking. Sometimes it's a miss but . . ." She looked at her daughter, silently reminiscing about an inside joke about a cooking mishap. "But she does pretty good. She'll be alright. Get better." She bobbed her head to reassure her. Her daughter smiled back at her mom sheepishly. Her mother's presence softened her.

I continued with her cross-examination, eliciting her testimony. As she spoke, I stole a glance at her daughter's defense counsel, who was smiling along with us, but obviously not paying attention to the conversation as it unfolded. If he had been, he wouldn't have realized how Tina's mother's testimony didn't match up with the defense.

A few jurors noticed what had evaded her lawyer. Their heads swiveled toward Tina, lingering there as their eyes moved from the mother to me. One placed her pen inside her notebook, closing it decisively before looking around the courtroom. The other flipped back a few pages, paused as she scanned the page, and then looked back at Tina. She exhaled sadly as she stared at the mother, pitying her.

There was no longer an alibi.

"Thank you. No further questions, ma'am."

She shifted in her seat, sitting up taller. She flashed a look at her daughter, reassured by what felt painless. Her daughter looked down, realizing what had gone wrong, closing her eyes. She used the back of her hand to wipe the tears that dripped from her jowl. Her mother stared at her, furrowing her brow, trying to understand her daughter's reaction.

"Tina?" she said from the witness stand. "What's wrong?"

The judge instructed her to step down from the stand.

"Tina," she repeated as she walked past the jury box, toward her daughter. "What happened? What's wrong?"

A marshal blocked her path, extending an arm to direct her out of the well.

Tina's mother looked at me pleadingly. "What happened? What happened? What did I say?"

My own daughter had quieted down, no longer moving within me. I touched my stomach, suddenly yearning for her response. I opened my mouth as if to respond by directing her toward the gallery, but reconsidered and looked to her daughter's attorney to weigh in. He told her he'd speak to her in a moment.

The judge's gavel sounded but had no effect.

"Love you?" she said directly to Tina, who smiled faintly. "Love you?" she implored, standing in the well.

I pressed my hand into my stomach trying to elicit a response from my daughter. A kick, a move, anything to know that she felt me.

"Love you," her daughter responded, mustering a smile.

Tina's lawyer handed her a tissue and quickly rubbed her back. Tina rebuffed him with an elbow shrug. Her co-defendant, Kim, never so much as looked in her direction. She stared stoically ahead, indifferent even to the sounds of her own children watching from the gallery. Tina's mother sat in the row behind her, leaning forward at the edge of the bench, waiting for her daughter to turn around.

Since all that was left in the trial were our closing arguments and it was already late afternoon, we agreed to resume in the morning to avoid disruption and allow the jury time to deliberate in the morning. None of us expected a lengthy deliberation, and we were indeed correct.

The next day, we wrapped closing arguments by 11:30 a.m. By 1:00, I was summoned back to the courtroom to receive the guilty verdict, read over the sounds of the defendants' children being shushed as they tried to get their mothers' attention.

Both women faced multiple years in prison. In the ringleader's case, the term was longer than the age of her children combined.

"Does the government request them to be held pending sentencing?"

"We do, Your Honor."

"I assumed as much." The judge looked pensive.

She extended a rare gift: "Prison time is warranted for this matter, but I see the children in the room, and I . . . am a mother myself. I will give you all an opportunity to settle your affairs and secure care for your children before I hand down my sentence. Please prepare yourselves—and your children—accordingly."

We rose for the judge's departure. I motioned for the victim to wait for me in the hall as I gathered my belongings. She opted instead to wait inside the courtroom to walk out beside me. She was alone with her daughter in her arms, trying to balance her baby on one hip and prevent the diaper bag from sliding off her arm toward the other. She kept trying to put the bottle back in the baby's mouth to soothe her.

She looked tired, anxious, afraid to be alone in the room. She hadn't expected the defendants to leave the courtroom with her that day, and the courageous bravado of her testimony dissipated as she recognized that nothing protected her but the words "restraining order," typed on a piece of paper stapled in the corner to an information sheet on how to contact police if the defendants violated it.

I offered to carry her bag, placing it on my rolling briefcase as we made our way out of the courtroom. She clutched it instead like a security blanket. "Look straight ahead," I told her, placing my hand on her back to show her she was not alone. We walked past family members teeming with a range of emotions. My colleague lingered with defense counsel, discussing another case.

"So what now?" she asked. We lingered in the hall while she filed through her bag in search of a tissue to wipe her baby's nose. The suspense of waiting for a verdict had led her to believe that the conviction would bring about something other than the anticlimactic feeling that lingered.

I looked inside my purse and handed her a small pack of tissues. "Now we wait to come back for sentencing. Are you going to be okay? Do you want me to have the detective drive you home?" I asked.

"Yes, no thank you, I'm fine." She laughed nervously before clarifying her answer: "Yes. Yes, a ride home would be good. I'm going to be fine. Will you tell him what happened?"

"Who? Your boyfriend? No, I assumed you'd tell him what happened. I'm not in contact with him."

"That makes two of us."

"Why? What happened?" I asked, watching her bounce his child in her arms. The man behind the jealous rage that had provoked the savage assault on her had been in prison since her second trimester. I wondered what had prompted her decision to stop talking to him now.

"I asked him about those jail calls you played. Between him and her," she explained. Interestingly, she reserved her venom for the word "her." "I didn't know they still talked like that. I broke up with him. We broke up. He keeps calling but I don't answer like that anymore. All this time I thought . . . like, she was lying . . . now I don't know what to think, you know?"

"Yes, I know." And I did. I knew precisely what to think. Not only had I heard the jail calls a month ago, I had also seen the videotaped visits between him and Kim. They were obvious lovers, and I'd heard him entice both women with the same sexual fantasy scripts on the phone. He had manipulated them both, reveling in the attention and commissary contributions of his two warring marionettes. For evidentiary reasons, we were limited by the court in our ability to play the extent and substance of conversations unrelated to the crime itself at trial. She had no idea of the full nature of his duplicity.

I couldn't warn her before the trial without risking tipping off Kim, since the victim would have undoubtedly confronted him about it, revealing crucial evidence in my case. The ringleader confessed on the calls while her children called him "Daddy" in the background. The jury, and the victim, only needed to hear the relevant admitted evidence and confession, not the full catalog of calls, at trial.

"I just gotta figure things out now, I guess. I thought he would be coming home soon, but he's not, anyway. And I was going to bring her up there to see her father. He said he couldn't get enough of the pictures. She looks just like him, he says." She did, and so did Kim's oldest daughter. I had heard him say how he couldn't get enough of her pictures in his cell, either.

The baby arched her back away from her mother and threw the bottle down. I leaned down to retrieve it and placed it back in her hand. She threw it down again, this time releasing the bottle cover. Milk splashed as the two pieces struck the floor.

"Someone needs a nap," I said, and signaled that I would grab it again. As I reached for it, the other part of the love triangle walked out of the double doors. Her shoe almost grazed the bottle before she caught herself and started to pick it up. Kim froze as she realized who its owner was. She looked at the victim, holding her baby girl. Her lawyer told her to wait, recalling the stay-away order that prevented the now-convicted ringleader from being within a hundred yards of the victim. She stared at the bottle and swallowed.

Her oldest daughter held her hand, and asked, "What's wrong, Mommy?"

Aware of the tension but ignorant of its roots or ramifications, the little girl bent down to pick the bottle up from the ground and carried it back to the baby bouncing on her mother's hip. The baby leaned down to smile at her happy face, squealing, which made the other girl giggle.

"Aww, she's a cute little baby!" she said, emulating the voice and intonations of a grown woman.

Two mothers, victims for different reasons, stared at the innocence of their daughters' interaction. One mother would go home to prepare a bath for her daughter and wonder whether to accept her child's father's call. The other would prepare her daughter for life without her incarcerated mother. I wondered if one day their paths would cross again. I hoped so.

After all, their little girls were sisters.

12

Grandstanding for Justice

On the Roles We Play Within the Grand Jury

The phone rang. I paused the breast pump, waiting a beat for the machine to stop before I answered.

"This is Laura Coates . . . alright . . . thank you. Which grand jury is it? How much longer are they serving? . . . okay . . . give me ten minutes, please. I've just got to finish one thing and I'll be right down."

I felt my breasts to see whether they had returned to a malleable state and were no longer taut and hardened by the swell of milk. I removed the nursing bra and leaned forward to ensure that the remaining drops within the tube would top off the bottles. Detaching the piping from my body, I carefully screwed the two bottle tops on, feeling the warmth of the milk through the plastic as I checked to see how many milliliters I had. I slipped them into the black thermal bag I kept next to my desk and placed the bag inside of the miniature black fridge under my window, swapping it for a bottle of water.

I hooked my thumbs under the straps of the bra that was nestled around my torso and slipped them over my shoulders, examining my button-down shirt to see whether the leaked milk stains had dried without a trace. Two yellowed circles stared back at me.

I remembered a spare shirt hanging on the back of my door. It was tighter and shorter than I remembered and taunted my waist as it crept higher toward my belly button. There was no time to change back into the other shirt, so I decided to button the suit jacket and made a mental note not to lift my arms. The jacket was now also ill-fitting but it would have to work.

Grabbing my case file, I scanned my desk to make sure that there was no trace of my breast pump on it and nervously reconfirmed that I had indeed placed my baby's liquid gold into the refrigerator. Then I unlocked the door, to be met instantly by the commotion of an office in motion. My office phone rang again. I checked my watch—it had likely already been ten minutes, and I knew it was the grand jury office threatening to give my time slot away. I opted for the stairs to avoid any further delay.

"I know, I know," I said, swooping past the office of the prosecutor assigned to manage the grand jury's schedule. I knew she was waiting to point out my tardiness, eager to give my assigned time slot to the next prosecutor who needed it. "Which one is it again?"

"You almost missed your spot. Everyone has been calling today to ask for a spot, Laura. You're not going to be able to go for very long. There's another prosecutor who needs to meet with that grand jury right after you!"

"Got it. I don't need much time today. Thanks for squeezing me in," I said, finally facing her as I used my back to push open the door to my assigned grand jury room.

"Hello, everyone!" I said cheerfully to the grand jury. "How is everyone doing today?"

"She's back!" shouted a middle-aged White man in a button-down shirt opened to a T-shirt underneath. He said it with a broad smile.

"We ate beforehand this time, Laura," a Black woman in her sixties chimed in. "We won't be hangry this time."

"Thank God!" I joked. "There's nothing worse than being the thing standing between you all and your lunch break."

"Did you eat, Laura?" another juror, a White woman in her sixties, asked. "Or do you need Mike to give you another one of those power bar thingies?"

I laughed at their memories. My stomach had relentlessly growled during my last presentation, and the man with the button-down had produced a bar out of pity. They didn't let me hear the end of it.

"I ate—and well!" I lied. I didn't have time to pump and grab lunch. Hopefully my stomach wouldn't give me away again.

I scanned the room, making eye contact with each juror. "Chris, I'm gonna need your headphones off for just a few minutes today." He was a White man in his twenties. Pretending to be annoyed, he took them off with a sigh.

"I don't know how you remember everybody's names, Laura," a young Black woman in her early twenties said, beaming. She was applying to law school and was evidently in awe of the process.

Grand jurors are just like any other members of the community who get called for jury duty, except that instead of being told to report for a particular trial to determine guilt or innocence, they are required to serve on a grand jury for weeks to determine whether a prosecutor has probable cause to charge an arrestee with a felony offense. Prosecutors don't need to prove anything beyond a reasonable doubt at this point, only that there is probable cause to believe that a crime was committed and that this person was the one to have done it. If the jurors believe there is probable cause, they can return an indictment that formally charges the defendant with one or more felony offenses. At trial, a separate pool of jurors will be assembled to hear the case and render a verdict.

Over the course of their term as grand jurors, they will subpoena and hear evidence and testimony in any number of cases, presented by a variety of prosecutors. Prosecutors will present evidence and witnesses as they become available, which can lead to sporadic scheduling. They may hear about a particular case on day one, and not again for several days or even weeks. Prosecutors help jurors keep track of their cases by assigning a number to each case.

"What case number is this for you today?" I directed my question to the man who never smiled. He had mentioned that he was a defense attorney by training.

"You're prosecutor number five today," he said dryly.

"Alright, well, I know there's someone coming after me, so let's get started. I've got a new case for you today. So this is—let me see—they told me this is now, what? The twenty-sixth case you'll be hearing, right? So let's call this one case number twenty-six. Is that right?"

"Correct," the man without the smile affirmed.

"What happened to the other one?" the playful hangry retiree asked. "The one with the mom and the two little girls?"

"Not today. I'll be back for that." She was disappointed not to have an update.

"So . . . what do you have for us today? Who did what to who and when?" A White man in his forties, my most prolific notetaker, was already putting his pen in position. "What kind of witness? Victim, I mean. Survivor, I mean."

"You won't be hearing from a witness today. Actually, we're going to do something a little new. The witness has already testified in front of the grand jury, just not you. The last one expired—I know you all can't wait for your term to end—and so I need to present her testimony to a new grand jury."

"Is it like a videotape or something? How are we gonna watch it?"

"Dammit, I *knew* I should've got that popcorn!" A White man in his early thirties, the resident jokester, had been waiting for his moment to deliver. His predictability never disappointed.

"No, no need for popcorn. But I do need a volunteer! Who's it gonna be?"

"I'll do it!" the jokester exclaimed. "It'll keep me awake." He walked toward me before he even knew what he had signed up for.

"Great. I was gonna have you play me, but I think I'll have you play the witness instead."

"Play the witness? What do you mean?"

I handed him a copy of the transcript.

"You and I are gonna act this out. I'll be me, and you be the witness. Believe me, it's better than reading it to ourselves. I have to get it on the record anyway."

"I've always wanted to do a scene study." He turned to the jurors and mockingly said, "What's, what's my motivation for the scene?" He got the laughter he sought, but it wasn't yet enough. "Am I pretty? Angry? What emotion am I giving? Oh, and can I sit in the witness chair?"

"Of course. I wouldn't have it any other way," I said agreeably, knowing his laughter would soon end.

The man without a smile crossed his arms with impatience.

We began.

I watched him change the tone of his voice, assuming a female affect. He believed she'd be indignant, ignorant, attitudinal, and self-righteous and played her precisely that way as we made our way through the oath and introductory testimony.

I admonished him not to ad-lib or assume details not in evidence. I knew that his craving for laughter wouldn't let him play it straight, but I kept him in line, honing in on his increasing discomfort with the facts as they were revealed.

177

"And what happened next?" I read from the transcript, already anticipating the weight of the revelation ahead.

"He kicked me between my legs and I felt like I had peed on myself . . ." He tried to scan the page before continuing with the affect.

"Please continue," I instructed.

He restarted, this time without the affect. "He kicked me between my legs and I felt like I had peed on myself. I tried to cover my stomach and block him but he kept kicking me."

"What happened when you fell down?" I read.

He stopped again, scanning the page as the color drained from his face.

"Please continue," I instructed.

"I . . ." He resumed. "He dragged me up by my hair and told me to stand and then he would punch me in the face so I would fall again . . ." He stopped.

"How many times did he punch you in the face?"

"I don't know. I couldn't see after the third one. I could feel my hair ripping out each time he lifted me."

He folded the pages toward each other and looked at me. "What did she look like?"

"Please continue," I said.

"I know, I know. I just . . . want to know what she looked like is all."

"What does it matter?" another juror asked.

"He just wanna know if she's White. You see he already tried to make her Black," another juror, a Black woman in her seventies, said, sucking her teeth. He wasn't funny anymore.

"Someone else wanna read?" he asked. "I, uh, I don't, uh . . . anyone else wanna read for her?"

"I'm going to take over from here," I interjected. "I'll read both. I remember the moment."

Something had triggered him. He couldn't get out of the chair fast enough. His lips were as tense as his body as he returned to his seat, blinking.

"Everybody okay?" I asked, not waiting for the answer.

I continued, playing both the role of the woman who was so savagely attacked and myself. I read her words the way I remembered her saying them, pausing when she paused and reading verbatim the description of her body movements.

"Let the record reflect, the witness is blotting her nose with a white Kleenex. The Kleenex has visible blood on it . . . Let the record reflect that she is bending over onto the desk sobbing; her shoulders are rising and falling as she is covering her head with her hands . . . Let the record reflect that her hands are shaking as she imitates the way he held the knife by wrapping her left hand around the pen in front of her and flicking it in the air in short bursts of motion . . . Let the record reflect that she is pointing to bald patches along her right hairline with a bandaged index finger . . ."

I allowed my voice to rise and fall as she had done. I distinguished between her and my own demeanor by sitting up straight and looking around the room to meet the eyes of the jurors and slumping vulnerably in the chair while hugging myself with one arm as she had done when she spoke.

As I read, the sounds of stifled tears escaped from several jurors. Reading her words aloud and channeling her pain provoked my own painful recollection of what it felt like to watch her choke on her words as she grappled with her fear and trauma. My eyes stung, and I reminded myself to repress my emotion to keep the focus on the victim I was portraying. But my body wouldn't let me be stoic. I felt my breasts, reacting to the sound of tears, preparing to lactate. I tugged at my lapel self-consciously, not wanting to draw attention to myself or to the fact that my body would not allow me to escape the weight of the moment.

"End of transcript," I said, uncrossing my leg and standing up, signaling that the role-playing had come to an end.

"Can we see what she looked like?" the regretful jokester asked again. "Not for anything about race. I just want to see who that happened to? Like, you know what I'm saying?"

It's always a curious thing, the need to see the victims. I wondered if he needed to see her to humanize her experience or if he simply wanted confirmation of his initial assumptions.

I signed into the laptop docked at the lectern and placed the photographs of her injuries on the screen.

The photographs were met with audible groans. One woman covered her eyes with her hand before looking again, only to cover her eyes again.

The jokester spoke first. "Did he explain why he did it?" I looked at him. "What I mean is—"

"I don't care what he has to say. There's no excuse to put your hands on a woman—on anybody like that," the man with the protein bar said, shaking his head.

A knock at the door interrupted us. I poked my head out to see the next prosecutor waiting to step in, and then I ducked back in.

"I'll be back tomorrow with the officer in this case, along with some additional requests. You'll hear from me about the potential charges, and I'll ask you to consider an indictment at the conclusion. Your next case is ready. Stretch your legs a minute. I'll see you tomorrow, okay?"

"Can we just vote to indict him right now?" my resident defense attorney spoke up.

"You haven't heard the rest of the story yet. As they say, 'But wait! There's more.' I'll see you sometime in the morning. Make sure you eat first."

I opened the door for the next prosecutor to tag in.

"Hi, everyone!" he said. "Uh-oh . . . Coates put you in a bad mood, didn't she? She wasn't talking about the Patriots again, was she?"

"Nah, they just like me better!" I winked, in recognition of this strategic moment of levity, and nodded to pass the baton.

"Is she really a Patriots fan?" I heard one juror say as the door closed behind me.

"You went over, Laura!" the clerk called after me as I walked past her office. I backtracked with a "sorry," leaning into her doorway.

"Does this mean I can't have a piece of candy?"

She laughed and pushed the bowl toward me. "Just one this time."

"Is that what happens when I don't pick up your call?" I joked.

"You answered my call," she said, without looking away from her computer.

"Oh, I thought you had called again just before . . . never mind. See you tomorrow!"

I walked into my office and made a beeline for the phone. I checked the missed call number as I dialed into voice mail.

It was the woman whose testimony I had just reenacted. She was begging for my help. The man who had savagely attacked her had come back. You could hear him screaming at her in the background to hang up the phone.

13

"The Chew"

On the Role of Privilege in Charging Decisions

The officer spat a brown liquid into the water bottle and rubbed the back of his mouth with his hand. The nauseating smell of chewed tobacco filled the air in an already claustrophobic space.

We were in a small room inside the satellite prosecutors' office in the basement of the courthouse, a disappointing reprieve from the row of officers lining the hall to speak with me about bringing charges against their arrestee. Its walls were cement blocks lined with mismatched filing cabinets covered in dust. Outdated telephone lists and court pamphlets were taped over one another on the wall. Empty discarded legal file folders were strewn on the carpeted floor, which held enough mold to antagonize my nasal passage with a vengeance.

Pen caps outnumbered pens, and the trash overflowed with lunch containers. There was no circulation; any stench hung like a fog. Bent blinds hinted at the outside world, but a window without a view could never prove its existence. We were trapped in a room where our feet alternately kicked wires or loose paper but none of us could stomach looking under a desk to remove the irritation. We kept our heads down, waiting for the chance to escape this dungeon and once again breathe fresh air.

"Do you have to do that in here?" I asked.

"Yeah. I do," the officer said. He was in his thirties. "Look, I've been up all night with this shit. Gimme a break."

"I mean, can you *maybe* use a darker bottle next time? So I don't have to actually see the chew spit?"

"Good idea," he said, spitting again. "Or *maybe* . . . you could hurry up and then we'd both go back to doing what we want."

"Asshole," I mumbled under my breath.

"What was that?"

I turned to him and raised my voice. "Oh, I called you an asshole." I cocked my head with a closed-mouth smile, blinking for emphasis.

He laughed. "Alright, alright. My girl says the same thing. Let's just get this done. I can smell myself anyway and want to take a shower. What else do you need from me?"

"Tell me what happened. Who said what now?"

"So two brothers were fighting over something stupid. One of 'em ate the last of the cereal, and it pissed the other one off."

"What kind of cereal?" I stopped, prepared to relate to his irritation, depending on the brand.

"Cocoa Puffs." We nodded, tilting our heads toward each other, jokingly pretending to validate the brother's anger.

"Uh-huh . . . go on," I said, as I typed my notes into the computer.

". . . they start fighting. At first, it's just fists. Then one grabs a knife, the other one a pan . . . Hold on . . ." He spat, turning his back for a second to shield his habit, raising his eyebrow when he turned around. "Better?"

He still had to wipe his lips, using his hand again.

I shook my head and smirked. "Such a gentleman. Keep going."

"So one grabs a pan. It still had some grease in it. And he flings it at his brother with the knife."

"Hot grease?" I turned my head toward him while still typing.

"Nah, it was from the night before. You know when it has the white part on top? I'm telling you, this house was already nasty. I mean, I couldn't even look in the bathroom." He spat again, disgusted by the recollection of the filth. I stared at him, waiting for him to see the irony. He blinked back. "What was I saying?"

"You were telling me how nasty . . . *they* were. Also about the grease," I reminded him, my fingers poised above the keyboard waiting for him to continue.

"Right. The grease got on his clothes, so that just made him madder. He came at him with the knife and cut him, slashed his arm."

"Which arm? Right or left?"

"Yup," he said, not actually answering the question.

"Right or left?" I repeat.

"Nah, both. He slashed down twice. Got one side and then when he turned away to run, got him on the back of the other side."

"How bad are the cuts?" I sipped my tea, smelling the lemongrass through the mouth of the plastic lid, hoping the scent would replace the stench of his discarded spit and the thickness in the room.

"Pretty bad. I have the pictures on my phone. Check it out. Down to the white meat."

He stood up, bending at the waist, and leaned toward me with his phone. "See that?" he said, thumbing through the images, the jagged cuts that revealed ripped flesh. The smell of tobacco and metal on his hands overwhelmed my tea.

"See that one?" As he pointed to a photo on his phone, I noticed cuts on his hand. They appeared fresh, like he had scraped against concrete repeatedly.

"Why are your knuckles cut up like that?" I asked.

He turned his hand inward, pulling his lips apart with a kissing sound. "Man, that's the other arrest. The one before this call. He stuck his finger in my face. Had to take him down. I'll tell you about that case after I do the paperwork."

"You haven't done the paperwork on that other case yet?" I bemoaned his slowness. "We could have cranked both out fast and you could be done."

"I'm not tryin' to rush. I need to get some more time this month."

"I thought you wanted to leave and take a shower?" I winced as I watched him spit again. Some of the spit missed the mouth of the bottle and ran down his hand.

He winked. "Ima leave and come back."

"Make sure I'm not waiting on you to get pretty, please. I'm trying to leave at a decent hour myself." I wanted to go home to my family. I assumed he wanted overtime pay. "Finish telling me what happened. And do you have a printout of the pictures somewhere yet? I'll need them. You have the knife, right?"

"Yup," he said, handing me a form as he leaned down to pick up the water bottle before sitting down with a grunt. He spat again, missing the mouth of the bottle a second time, and he tried to wipe the spittle off the next set of paperwork he handed me.

"You know this is a disgusting habit, right?" I said, pinching the corner of the page as I held it up, not wanting to touch what had come from his mouth.

"For fuck's sake, man. You sound like my girl."

"I'm surprised you still have a girl with that habit!" I laughed, curling my lip back as I shook my head. "Seriously," I continued. "This is more disgusting to see than the pictures you showed me."

"Are we almost done? I'm not feelin' the lecture today, Coates."

"You tell me! You gonna bring me the next case before or after the shower?" I retorted, exaggerating the indignation I felt.

"Anyways," he continued, ignoring my question, "what else you wanna know?"

"Who called the police?"

"The girlfriend called the police."

"There's a 911 call, right? You got a radio run, too?"

"Yup. We responded to it."

"So, where is the victim now? Did the ambulance come?"

"Yup. He went to the hospital, getting stitches."

"Is he still there?"

"Don't know." He spat again, scraping his lip with his teeth.

"Where's the girlfriend—wait, she's which one's girlfriend? I guess I shouldn't try to assume."

"The victim's girlfriend. The one who got stabbed. She called the police."

"Alright, that's what I thought. Let me make sure I made that clear . . . hold on." I quickly but softly read back my notes aloud, skimming the irrelevant details as I searched for the reference to the girlfriend. "Got it. Did the defendant make any statements?"

"Yeah, I laid it out in the paperwork. He admitted it. Tried to say it was self-defense over the grease, but uh-uh." He started to chuckle, leaning in to tell me a joke he was sure I'd get a kick out of. "He wanted me to arrest him for the grease on his shirt. I'm like, you stabbed him over a shirt—you kept stabbing him as he ran—and you want me to crisscross an arrest cuz you got oil on you? Nah, man. Had someone actually cleaned in that nasty-ass house, you wouldn't have had that problem in the first place." He laughed, spitting into the bottle again, and then paused, saying, "Hold on, I gotta get another bottle. This one's getting full, and I see this is gonna take a minute."

"Seriously? Just wait a second. I'm almost done. Swallow it if you have to, for Christ's sake."

"You don't swallow it. That's nasty," he said, disgusted.

"Oh *that's* what's nasty?" I scratched the back of my neck and uncrossed my leg to get closer to the desk. I gripped the center drawer to pull myself in, yanking the drawer open as I moved. Unraveled paperclips and sugar packets peppered the compartments. Something made a crunching sound as I tried and failed to reclose the drawer. Bowing my head to look inside to remove the obstruction, I found an empty water bottle. I shook the drawer to get it to close.

"What's the problem?" the officer asked. "What's stuck?"

"Someone left a water bottle in here. Why, I don't know."

"Lemme get it," he said, reaching his hand inside the drawer. The plastic crunched again as he wriggled it out of the shallow drawer. He held it up like a trophy. "Looks like I've got a new bottle."

I shook my head at his singular focus and couldn't help but laugh. "How lucky for me."

He unscrewed the new bottle, lining the bottom with a fresh round of brown spit.

"Is the victim cooperative?" I said, refocusing.

"For now."

"Alright, well, let's see if he really is. Let's call him now. What's the number?" I scanned the paperwork and dialed the number three digits at a time, checking the screen to confirm that what I was entering was correct.

I turned my back to the officer as he held up the new bottle to show me how full it was getting, peeking back playfully out of the side of my eye as I waited for the victim to pick up.

"Hello?" A tired man's voice muffled through the receiver.

I hit the speakerphone button and replaced the handset on the base. The cord retwisted around itself slowly as it lay there. I replied, "Yes, hi. This is Laura Coates. I'm an Assistant United States

Attorney for the District of Columbia. I'm sitting here with an officer. I understand you might be at the hospital right now. How are you feeling?"

"Um, fine," he said, hesitating. He started speaking in hushed tones to someone in the background. The mouthpiece scraped audibly against his chin. "I don't . . . it's the police . . . I know . . . right . . . no, it's a female."

I bristled at being called a female. It always sounded like I was a non-human species being studied at a zoo.

"Okay, hello?" He returned to the phone.

"Hello. Forgive me for eavesdropping there, but I'm actually not the police. I'm sitting here *with* the police, though—the officer who was at your home last night."

The officer mouthed the words "yesterday, not night."

"Excuse me, yesterday, I mean. Not the night. Yesterday. When you and your, um, brother—" I searched for the defendant's name on the paperwork.

The officer mouthed "Chris" and then stood up to drag his finger under the name on the paperwork. "Chris," he mouthed again. The water bottle was too close to my arm, and I shrugged my shoulder away.

"—Chris," I continued. "Your brother, Chris. I wanted to understand if you were interested in pursuing charges against your brother, Chris." I looked at my sleeve, confirming that the bottle had not left a mark on my clothes. The officer pursed his lips and rolled his eyes.

"I mean, I kinda don't, um. I mean, I don't know. The officer told me you'd call. What?" he said, addressing a woman in the background. "Alright, look, do what you're gonna do. I'm not sure what else to say about it."

"Are you still at the hospital?"

"No, I'm back home."

"Is that your girlfriend in the background?"

"Yeah, she's here."

"Okay, well, please feel better. I'm going to ask for a restraining order so he can't come back to the house while you're there, okay? Would that be helpful to you?"

"That means he can't come back here today or for twenty-four hours or something like that?"

"Yes, exactly, he can't come near you, your home, or your place of employment or anything like that. It's not forever, but the assigned prosecutor will contact you soon and give you more details, okay?"

"So you gonna go forward with the case? You're gonna charge him, right?"

"Yes." I purposely didn't elaborate; I wanted to avoid being locked into a particular charge. I was still deciding which one fit, but at least I knew I had a cooperative victim. Frankly, we could still prosecute even if he was reluctant, but it makes the prosecution that much harder. I annotated my notes to reflect that he was amenable to charges. The prosecutor who would be assigned this case would need to work quickly before he changed his mind. "Someone will be in touch with you soon, okay? Thank you!"

"Alright," he said, skipping the goodbye.

I picked up the handset and put it down again to end the call and then turned to the officer, repeating what he'd already heard.

"He's at the house. Sounds like his girlfriend's with him. What was she like?"

"Oh, the girlfriend? Yeah, she's pissed. Made all kinds of statements. A little bit reckless."

"Are you gonna be able to serve the witness and the victim with subpoenas today? I mean, you could do it tomorrow."

"Yup," he said with a wink. "I'll do it right before my shower . . . today. And then I'll come back and tell you about these knuckles." He spat into the bottle again.

"Get out, and take the nastiness with you, please." I pointed to his two bottles, handing him the file to pass to the next prosecutor, who would complete the paperwork. Despite the fact that I was freezing, I turned on the fan in the corner to air the room out before I called in the next officer.

Today I was only screening cases, deciding whether to go forward with charges ("paper" the case) or not pursue charges ("no paper" the case and ignore the arrest). My decision was supposed to be final. There were nearly one hundred people on the lockup list. They had been arrested within the last twenty-four hours and were in holding cells awaiting their fate. Either they would be released without being charged or they would soon be facing a judge arraigning them on a charge.

The arresting officers who lined the hallway outside the prosecutors' office in the basement of the courthouse were in various states of fatigue. They had come off their shifts, and this was the last thing standing in the way of clocking out. Some leaned back against the wall, sleeping uncomfortably, their body contorted. Others swapped stories about the night before, comparing war wounds on their bodies or photos on their phone.

Someone had brought in a few boxes of doughnuts, and officers picked through them, looking for their jolt of sugar that would keep them awake. They gathered around the counter, leaning on one elbow as they signed documents. Another group stood around the copier, offering suggestions as a prosecutor knelt beside it, trying to find the source of the jam. The other copier was broken, again. This would surely delay everything, again.

A group of prosecutors sat in desks surrounding my temporary office, waiting to see which cases I decided to paper so they could prepare files for the assigned prosecutors. After I gave the go-ahead, they would do the heavy lifting, working with the officers to ensure that the police paperwork was complete, with all *i*'s dotted, all *t*'s crossed. They compiled the evidence: officers' notes, crime scene photos, and chain of custody information for the physical evidence. For each case, they prepared all documents in possession of the officer and put together a packet of information that would be presented to the defense counsel as initial discovery at arraignment even before the assigned prosecutor saw the file. They made requests for the 911 call and created subpoenas for witnesses. They would even write a letter to the defense counsel presenting an initial plea offer to resolve the case. All within thirty minutes of the officer's leaving my dungeon cell that now smelled like tobacco and musk.

Whatever information these prosecutors missed would impact the office's ability to go forward and prosecute the case. The sheer volume of cases and the officers' inability to remember so many cases, let alone distinguish between similar cases, often made it impossible for the assigned prosecutor to track down whatever might be missing from a file. Notes got lost. Paperwork, too. Witnesses couldn't be located. A wrong address or misspelled name could change the warrant. It had to be perfect, but there was just no time for it to be.

I stood up to stretch, feeling the life coming back to my legs as the muscles elongated. I placed my palms along my lower back as it pulled across the back of my hip, and I grimaced in pain. I exhaled, letting my limbs dangle for a moment while I watched the fan swirl the cobwebs hanging between the file cabinets as the fan head rotated, jerking to a pause at each end of the path.

I checked my phone. My husband had sent a picture of my family at home, and I called to check in.

"Hey." I heard the chaos in the background as he pushed hands away from the phone, saying, "Wait, hold on, lemme talk to Mommy." A rookie mistake to say "Mommy." He paid for it.

"Mommy?" I heard the sound of little hands wrestling the phone from his ear. "Mommy? Mommy, where are you? When are you coming home?"

I peeked into the hallway. There were at least twenty more cases to screen, and there was always the possibility that more would be added to the list before the workday was done.

"Soon, baby. Are you being a good girl?"

"Yeah . . . but I want you to come home now."

"I know, honey. Me too. But I bet you guys are having so much fun with Daddy! Where's your brother?" I said, changing the subject.

"He's playing with his . . . his toy. When did you say you were coming home?" She was persistent. We both knew I hadn't given her a time.

"How about if I bring you a special treat?" I dangled a distraction.

"What kind of a treat?" she said, delighted but skeptical.

I scanned the room for inspiration but found none.

"A special one!" I hedged, unsure of what I would be able to find, knowing it might end up being the fruit snacks in the vending machine in the hall. I wondered if I even had cash.

"Yay! Mommy said . . . ," she said, dropping the phone to go find her brother. She relished a chance to break the news, wasting no time doing it: "Mommy's gonna bring us a special treat now. She's coming home now!"

"No, no, wait—not home yet. That's not what Mommy said!" I called after her. I knew she'd already lost interest. I called my husband's name to get his attention, hoping he was still close by to at least end the call.

He heard me and picked up the phone. "I hope you weren't still talking to her. You know she's already moved on. When are you coming home? You promised her a treat?"

"It'll be a while still. Not sure how many of these cases will actually get papered, but there's been a lot so far. Depends on how fast everyone feels like moving. A lot of felonies today." I sighed. "I gotta go, okay? Thanks for the pictures! Keep 'em coming, love."

I stuck my head back out into the hallway and called the next officer, a White woman in her late thirties. She smiled and asked how I was doing.

"Not as tired as you, I'm sure. Whaddya got for me?" I said, sitting down.

"You're hot in here?" she asked, looking at the fan.

"No, I was trying to air it out in here. Your boy was spitting his chew."

She laughed. "I don't even smell that stuff anymore."

I turned off the fan. The heat barely made a dent on a good day. The fan being on had just set the temperature back, and it would be at least an hour before I felt warm again.

She handed me a case and sighed. I grabbed it with one hand and wrapped my scarf around my neck with the other.

"This is a no paper, but the victim really wants to talk to you. I tried to tell her."

"What's the case about?" I asked, curious about her certainty of my decision, as I billowed my scarf away from my throat.

She yawned as she spoke, covering her mouth at the end with a fist. "Two girls met at their off-campus apartment. One White. One Black. One shoved the other."

I wondered why she shared their races. I waited for her to elaborate.

"And . . . is that it?" I asked, waiting for the reason she was here.

"And she's upset about getting shoved by her roommate." She moved her hands up and away from each other like a conductor directing the orchestra.

"That's it? You've got to be kidding me."

"I wish I was." She yawned again, chewing the air twice as she closed her mouth.

"Did someone get hurt?" I felt like I was pulling teeth.

"I mean, I didn't see anything, really. But she showed me a scratch on her face and a little redness under her bra strap."

"Okay . . . well, is the scratch bad?" I typed notes as she spoke.

"It's really like a raised welt, which doesn't even make sense if she was shoved on her chest. I couldn't be sure it even came from today. I'm telling you. I told her. But she is adamant. She wants to talk to you about it." I couldn't tell if we were on the same page. Was she trying to make the case or not make the case?

"What happened before the roommate shoved her? Any claim of self-defense?" I needed to consider all angles, even if I already felt justified in my decision not to paper.

"They were yelling at each other and the other girl was trying to walk away and go into her own room, but she told her she wanted her out and started throwing her stuff in the hallway. The other girl got mad because the other one kept blocking her from walking away and so she shoved her out of her way, apparently pretty hard, knocking her into a table. The lamp broke. So she's pissed about that, too."

"Wait! You arrested the other girl for this? Why?"

"Yeah, they had some kind of beef from before, so I've been there. The one she shoved pays more in rent or something like that, and now the one who she shoved away—well, she says she feels like she's in danger now or whatever, so she wants a protective order against the roommate who shoved her." She was as annoyed as I was by the amount of energy spent on this conversation, deciphering which roommate was which, but she didn't answer why she arrested the roommate. I pressed.

"So . . . why did you arrest the roommate?" I reached my tongue back to feel my top molar.

"In a domestic, you know someone's gotta go. And she was the one to actually lay her hands on someone, so . . ."

"Even though she was trying to just leave and get the woman out of her way?"

"Someone had to go," the officer repeated. "She wants a protective order, too, even when you no paper this." She had already expected me not to charge this case.

"So, walk her through how to get a protective order from the court, separately."

"Nope. She wants to talk to you. She says there are other issues and wants to be able to throw the other girl out."

"Well, we don't do evictions. Why are you even entertaining this? You see that line of officers outside?"

"I know. What's worse is she changed her story twice, by the way. I don't believe either of 'em."

"Believe either of 'em—you mean either of the stories, or either of the girls?"

"Oh, sorry! I don't believe either of the stories the victim told."

"Did you write that somewhere in your notes?"

"Yup." That was the nail in the coffin. There would be no way to successfully prosecute this when the arresting officer didn't believe the victim.

"Okay, so obviously I'm not going to charge this case."

"Told you," she said, twisting her head quickly to show her prediction was correct.

I started to print out the paperwork that codified my decision not to proceed with this case when the officer mentioned something as if it were an aside. "She wants to talk to you. She's gonna keep calling us until she hears it from someone else. Just do me a favor and talk to her."

"Alright, I'll call and explain why we're not papering this foolishness. Where's her number?"

"No, no. She's here. She wants to talk to you."

"Where? In the building? How?"

"She wanted to talk to you."

"So you brought her here? Come on." I could barely hold my head straight processing her stupidity. Suddenly I preferred the spitter to her nonsense.

"Look," she said, throwing up her hands in defeat.

"Look what? I'm not papering this case. Go let her know I'm too busy to talk to her in person. That's not a waiting room."

"I'm telling you. She's gonna wait."

"So let her wait. You should have explained it to her yourself."

"Alright . . . ," she said, anticipating the response. "I'm telling you, I'll be right back."

"Can you just send in the next person, please?" I said to her back as she walked outside. My head could not stop shaking with disbelief. I waited for a moment, but no one entered.

I slapped my thighs as I stood up to look into the hallway to call the next person.

Through the window over the counter, I spotted the officer explaining the decision to a twenty-something blonde who was aggressively screaming back at her. The officer tipped her head as the blonde repeatedly poked her finger into the officer's chest, shouting something inaudible from within the office. I watched for a moment, waiting for a commensurate response that never came. I remembered the spitting officer's bloodied knuckles after being similarly provoked.

I shook my head as the officer raised her hands out of her pockets only to tuck her thumbs into the waistband behind her belt buckle. She bobbed her head dismissively as the blonde's poke pushed her body slightly backward. The officer held out her hand in protest and gestured with her thumb toward my office.

An officer walked through the door beside her, inviting the sounds from the hallway inside, so I could overhear, "It's her decision. You're welcome to talk to her about it."

"What's her name? She needs to, she's required to talk to me! Excuse me—*move!*" When the officer blocked her from storming through the door, she turned instead to the window. She smacked the window with her hand, shouting through glass that muted her. She screamed at the officer again, throwing her drink on the ground.

Even if I had just been reluctant to address her immediately, I was certain I would not now. I beckoned the next officer into my office.

His case was gruesome but paled in comparison to the gore of the next. The next two were crisscrossed defendants. Neither could be proven to have been the instigator. The next, a warrant case for a serial rapist. Then, a sustained beating of a transgender prostitute. Still ahead was a mistress discovered and burned with a cigarette. Another, a man strangling his ex-boyfriend with his own belt. The next two were slaps. I finished the last three and waited for the spitting officer to return from his shower.

The blonde woman was still waiting, now pacing on her phone. Surprisingly, the officer who had brought her here was still waiting to speak with me again. "Ready to get poked again?"

"Such a bitch," she said. I paused. "Her, not you," she clarified.

Out of deference to the officer, I decided to end her purgatory. I asked the officer to escort me outside to speak with the woman.

I stepped outside to find a brown liquid pooling on the ground beside her. I suppose she expected someone else to clean up the drink she had angrily slammed down an hour before.

"How can I help you?"

"How can you help me? You can charge my fucking case, that's how. I've been waiting out here forever. This is important."

She had no idea what important looked like in the grand scheme of things.

"So, first. Don't swear at me. Or shout. It's a courtesy that I'm even standing here. Let's try this again. How can I help you?"

She collected herself for just a moment before escalating again. "Why won't you charge her? She assaulted me! Do you see my face? Look at my face!" She pointed to an invisible mark under the wrong eye.

"I don't see anything there. But I understand this happened some time ago today. The officer didn't see anything visible other than a welt on the other side of your face. Is that what you're referring to?"

"I don't care what you can see, dammit! I want her out of my house!" She was actually stomping her feet. She seemed like a caricature.

"Okay, let me give you a number you can call about securing assistance with an eviction and also a temporary protective order. I'm assuming you own the property?"

"Own it? I'm renting! I'm like twenty. I'm still in college!"

"Okay, so who is on the lease?"

"We're both on the lease. So what! It was my place first and I let her move in so technically it was mine first so . . . I just want her gone. Do you get it?"

"Well, you'll have to speak with your landlord about how they want to handle the lease termination. They'll let you know what's possible and what's not. But here's a number that will give you some information on who is the appropriate contact. I understand you also want to do a protection order because you feel unsafe?"

"I thought I couldn't get one unless you charge her!" She looked at the officer mockingly.

"That's not correct. A criminal case is not always required. When you call, they can walk you through the requirements."

"So you're just not gonna help me?"

"I am helping you. I'm giving you the information you need to reach the right resources to solve the problems you have."

"Is this because you think I'm racist?"

"Excuse me?" I said, looking over at the cop. She shook her head, rolling one eye and fluttering the eyelid.

"This is what I've been dealing with," the officer said, waving her hand in front of the blonde.

"The cop thinks I am. She thinks I just keep calling because she's Black. But I've been assaulted. I would have called if she were purple. I don't care about her being Black. It's not just that she's Black. Not that she's Black at all. I mean, yes, she is Black. Very Black. She is that. And obviously I'm White. But that's not why I'm here. I don't care about her being Black. That's irrelevant, you understand. What matters to me is that I get justice. She assaulted me. It doesn't matter to that she's Black at all. I shouldn't have to live like this!"

"Ma'am, I made my decision based on the facts you presented to the officer, along with the inconsistent statements you made, the absence of injury, and her claims of self-defense and issues of your provocation. Frankly, I'm surprised they even arrested your roommate." I turned to the officer, raising my eyebrow.

She shrugged her shoulder.

"What the hell is that supposed to mean, inconsistent statements? What the hell is she talking about?" She directed her ire at the cop again.

I had already indulged this too long. "Do you have any other questions? For me?" I specified.

"What do I need to say to make sure you charge her the next time I call?"

I blinked at her.

"If you are assaulted, you should call 911 and get help from law enforcement. Anything else?"

"Is there a supervisor I can speak to? Someone . . . else?"

"Sure. Let me see who can make time for you." I already knew my decision would be final. The officer's written confirmation of her lack of credibility further guaranteed that this case was going nowhere, but I wanted to witness her hearing it confirmed.

"Can they come right now? I don't feel like waiting for it to take as long as it took you to do your job."

"Oh, of course," I said, sarcastically. "You're obviously our number one priority. I'll make sure they know that."

I went to find the person overseeing the case screening, a veteran White prosecutor in his fifties. I didn't ultimately report to him, as he was not my direct supervisor. But in his role today, he was the person intended to address and resolve any relevant concerns. He was sitting with an officer, working through some paperwork. I apologized for the interruption. "Hey! The woman standing at the counter says she was shoved by her roommate. No injury. The officer says she's lying but still arrested the other girl. She desperately wants the case papered. I said no. She wants to talk to someone else. Would you like me to tell her to wait for you?"

"Who, the blonde?" he said, peering over glasses. He stood up before I finished the details. "I'll speak to her," he said, pushing his paperwork aside for a moment. He didn't so much as excuse himself, even though the officer he was with was clearly trying to finish.

I followed him outside to the hallway and introduced him with a wave of my hand.

"Oh my. What seems to be the problem? You were assaulted by your roommate. She shoved you? I'm so sorry." The tone of his voice was cavity-inducing.

"Yes," she said, practically whimpering. Her tone had softened, and she suddenly appeared coquettish. "And no one cares. No one cares at all. I mean, I've been trying to explain to both of them, and they've just been so rude about everything. I've just been sitting her just asking for information and they're just laughing at me and being really aggressive and just rude."

"This must have been traumatizing for you. I'm so sorry."

The officer and I looked at each other in surprise, blinking. We were increasingly annoyed by the charade.

"My roommate. She's so scary. I mean, I don't know how much more I can take. I've never done anything to her. She just hates me for some reason. You should see her. See the way she looks. The way she looks at me. She just looks evil. You know what I mean?"

"I do. Well, why don't we see what we can do to help you. It's just not right. I'm sure we didn't understand how strongly you felt or how much this hurt you when we made our decision initially. But nothing is set in stone."

"Actually, my decision is . . . set in stone. We didn't fail to understand. She failed to tell the truth," I said, and then turned to the officer. "Officer, you made the statement that she told you two different stories. What did you mean by that?"

"I mean that she lied. Told me one thing when we first got there. And then when her roommate explained, she changed her story and said something else happened. It seemed pretty clear to me that she was just trying to say what she thought would get her arrested." I guess the officer remembered that poke in her chest after all. I was still trying to understand why she had even arrested the roommate, if that's the way she felt.

"I'm sure things got lost in translation," he continued, striking a tone that made my skin crawl. He turned to me. "I think we really might have to do something about this. She's very upset."

"I'm aware of that," I said, defiantly noncommittal.

She looked back at him. "Thank you," she said. "You have been really so sweet about this."

"Let me give you my card," he said, looking down as he spread his wallet. "Trust me. I'll take care of it for you." I wondered what he meant. It would get dismissed outright, serving no purpose other than to create a record for the roommate, who inexplicably had been arrested just to appease this young woman's unjustified indignance. But perhaps that was precisely the indelible mark she wished to stamp, and she had found a dupe eager to help her imprint it.

The blonde tucked her hair behind her ear and raised her eyebrow at me with a smirk as she looked over the top of my colleague's bowed head. Her expression switched back into that of a damsel in distress as he looked up to meet her gaze.

"It's always a privilege to get to speak to the people we serve."

"No, it was really my privilege," she said.

She was right.

14

I Just Don't Believe in It!

On the Tension Between Illegal and Wrong

"I'm not taking that case. *No!* It's ridiculous! I am so not doing this case! I'm sorry, but you're gonna have to take this case," my colleague Rebecca said, storming into my office in a fury, holding a file in her outstretched hand. She shook it, waiting for me to take it.

"What do you mean? What case?" I said, staring at the file.

"*This* case. I'm sorry! I just don't believe in these kinds of cases! I think they are so wrong. I just don't agree with them. I can't."

"I'm going to place this file in my hand, but it does not mean I'm taking it . . . understand?" I smiled, curious what could possibly be so repugnant.

I looked at the file, skimming the case summary. I looked up. "You can't take a rape case? Which part don't you believe in, exactly? The rape or the rape?"

"No, shut up. I obviously believe in prosecuting rape cases. I can't do statutory rape cases. It's just, I can't."

"Is there more to the story? What exactly is being charged? How old is the defendant?" I scanned the paperwork, sliding my index finger across the page, looking for the date of birth.

"A teenager. He's basically a teenager."

"And how old's the victim?"

"The same. She's young, too."

"So . . . why do we have this case?" I said, handing her back the file. She put her hands up and backed away dramatically.

"Nope. I'm telling you. I'm not taking this case. We shouldn't be prosecuting teens for having sex. Please."

"It says here he's twenty and she's, what, thirteen—wait, no, twelve. You don't see an issue with that?"

"You see an issue with that? Really? Come on, we were both teenagers. Stop it."

"Is she saying it was consensual? I mean, technically speaking she can't give consent, given her age . . . Is she saying it was forced?" I kept thumbing through the file, looking for the officer's notes.

"She says it happened at his house. In his basement."

"Did he bring her there? What's wrong with you? Why are you so anti this case?"

"Oh, come on. She knew him. I'm sure the parents walked in and that's it, and then she had to figure out how not to get in trouble. You know what I mean?"

"No, I don't."

"Whatever. Yes, you do," she said, dismissing my response. "He just turned twenty. I'm not doing this case. I already asked to give it away. It doesn't even make sense for me to keep it since I'm leaving this section soon anyway. So"—she clapped her hands—"congratulations! It's officially yours."

"Oh, gee, thanks so much!" I said, picking up the file and dropping it down like a weight for effect.

"Oh, and the girl is coming in today to meet with you. After school. I had asked Chelsea to do the interview because I wasn't gonna be here, so call her and just let her know. She may wanna stay on with you, but I'm done. Sorry!" She glided out of my office, closing her door down the hall when she got to her office.

I looked at the clock and wondered how long she'd had the file. I had been sitting in my office all day and had talked to her twice today. Why was she only just telling me now?

I called our colleague Chelsea. "So apparently I now have *that* case with you?"

"You do? Oh my God. Did Rebecca give you the same spiel about not being able to take teen sex cases?"

I laughed. "Yup. How ridiculous. I don't get her."

"You mean you don't like her. Oh wait, that's my opinion." She laughed. "Have you read the file? I literally just brought it back to her office. I see she walked it straight over to you after."

"Barely. I was just calling to see if there really was a meeting this afternoon with her? Please tell me there's not."

"Yup. In about an hour. Your girl scheduled this, not me. Her parents are coming, too."

"Bring me up to speed on what I've missed so far."

"I'll come down to you. Hold on."

"No, wait. I'll come to you. I need to walk. Just give me like thirty minutes to review everything so I know what's going on."

I hung up the phone and read through the file, trying to antici-pate how the jury might receive the information. The girl alleged no use of force, but the parents described an older man manipulating their impressionable daughter into engaging in sex acts. They were certain that he had been preying upon her naivete. The defendant worked near her elite private school. The officer's notes suggested that he might have an intellectual disability. Something about the story made me uncomfortable, and I was skeptical about how a juror might process it.

I checked the clock. It had been forty minutes since I'd spoken with Chelsea, and I had to fill in the blanks before I met with the victim. I wanted to be on the same page for our meeting with the victim. I stood up, fumbling with my heels as I tried to slide my feet back inside them. I grabbed my legal pad and a pen and walked down to Chelsea's office, stomping the foot that had fallen asleep.

I knocked on her half-open door, pushing it open as I peeked inside.

"So did she say 'we were both teenagers' to you, too?"

"Ha! Yes," I said, shaking my head. "How many people has she tried to pass this off to?"

"Who knows. Honestly, I'm happy to have you do the meeting, but I'm curious about this girl. It's not entirely clear what happened here."

"What do you mean?"

"I mean it seems like everything's come from the parents so far. They told the police what happened. They declined an exam on her behalf. Also, and I'm just guessing here—seems like they're not too pleased that he's Black."

"Did they actually say that or—"

"Yeah, I don't know. I wouldn't be surprised if that's part of it. Anyway, I think something happened, but I haven't heard from her directly yet. Her parents were very concerned and kept telling me she was too traumatized to speak to me. They've rescheduled twice already. I think the father is some kind of big shot. Not that it matters—but I'm just telling you the attention that might be on the case."

"Got it. So you want to take the lead on questions, or should I?"

"It's not like I've formed some kind of bond with her yet. But either way. Let's see who she responds to more and go from there. It's odd. I'm not usually skeptical about these cases. Maybe it's the way it first came to me. but I feel like my guard is up on this one, which I hate."

"I know what you mean," I responded. "My first impression is that this might be hard to prosecute, and I've been trying to change my mind ever since. Or, really, keep an open mind."

The phone rang. Security was calling to let us know that the girl and her parents had arrived.

From her parents' description, I was expecting a shrinking violet, someone as socially awkward as she was naive. I didn't have any idea of what she might look like, but I imagined that her energy would be that of a child traumatized by the manipulation of a domineering silver-tongued predator.

Which is not who we met. Instead, I introduced myself to a terse-lipped girl my height. When they weren't looking, she rolled her eyes while her parents talked. She didn't answer to confirm when they ended their sentences with "right?" She just looked off to the side and blinked slowly, shaking her head in annoyance. Her mother wrapped her arm around her shoulders, trying to push her daughter's cheek into the side of her bosom. I wondered if she noticed that her daughter was pulling her head away.

Her father spoke with an accent I couldn't place, his tone deliberately soothing, as if he hoped to endear himself to us. "We are obviously so overwhelmed and concerned. We feel like we have been hit with a truck. My wife is so upset. My daughter has hardly spoken, she's been so inconsolable about all of this."

The girl rolled her eyes again and stared at me, irritated. I fought not to glance over at Chelsea, though I already knew what she was thinking.

"Well, I'm so sorry to hear how this has really impacted your family. This is something no one can prepare for," I offered before he interjected.

"Exactly . . . exactly." He touched his wife's back. "I travel so much that I can't be home as much as I'd like, but now I've canceled everything. I told them, 'This is my daughter and she needs me.'"

She rolled her eyes again.

"Well," I began again. "We'd really like to speak to your daughter directly."

"Alone," Chelsea added.

"Yes, alone for a bit. It can be, um, difficult to have these conversations, but I do think it would be more comfortable for her."

Her mother turned to her, holding her shoulders on both sides. She bent her knees slightly to be at eye level with her daughter. "Are you okay talking to them by yourself? You want Mommy to be here with you?" she asked. She seemed to sincerely believe that she was not being patronizing.

"I'm fine," her daughter said, uttering her first words since her arrival.

Chelsea and I closed the door to the conference room, creating a barrier between us and her parents. We sat close to her at the end of the conference table.

Chelsea spoke first: "Seems like you wanted to get away from your parents for a second."

"Yeah," she said.

Chelsea continued, "Do you want to tell us how you're doing?"

She looked at her. "Do you have a boyfriend?"

Chelsea shook her head. "No."

"But you do," she said, pointing to my ring.

"I'm married."

"Is he Black?" she asked.

"Yes. He is."

"Can I see his picture?"

"You don't believe me?" I smiled.

210

"I just want to see him."

I pulled up a picture on my phone. "That's him," I said.

"He's cute. You and me like the same type."

"Type? You have a type already?" It was obvious I would be taking the lead from here.

"I know what I like."

"And what do you like, exactly?"

"I don't know. Cute. Tall."

"That's a short list."

She shrugged. I waited for her next statement, sure one was coming.

"Are you guys really gonna ask me about all this?" She looked at both of us.

"Yes. Why don't you tell us what happened that night? Start with how you know him."

"He works near my school and I see him outside sometimes."

"How did you end up talking?"

"One day I saw him outside on his break, standing in the parking lot and I was waiting to get picked up, so, you know. We started talking like that."

"And did he ask for your number or something?"

"I asked for his and I gave him mine. He seemed like he wasn't gonna ask, so I did."

"Did he know how old you were?"

"I told him I was a senior. Eighteen."

"Did he believe you?"

"Yes. He seems like, he's like . . . I mean, he's really cute, but he seems young or something." I remembered the words "intellectual disability" written in the officer's notes.

"Did you know how old he was?"

"Yes."

"And how often did you talk on the phone?"

"I mean, for a while, but we texted too."

She described how their conversations began as casual flirtations but quickly became increasingly sexual, graduating to a scheduled time to have sex. "He seemed like he didn't understand at first, like, what I wanted, but eventually I spelled it out for him. Like what I wanted to do. With him." She had set the tone and the pace.

"Is that how you ended up at his house?" Chelsea asked.

"Yeah. He told me to come over that night," she said, referring to the evening under investigation. "Like, after my mom went to sleep."

"So he picked you up?"

"No, I took a bus to the Metro and then walked."

"At ten o'clock at night?" I looked at her, surprised this story hadn't ended differently.

"I got there and he snuck me in through the basement door."

"And then what happened?"

She described how they kissed for a short while before moving on to intercourse. She was only naked from the waist down. He only removed his shirt and unzipped his pants. He wore a condom that she provided. It lasted less than five minutes, on a futon with a Superman fitted sheet hanging off the side. He told her to start getting dressed right away and started texting on his phone. She was lacing up her shoes when his mother opened the door to the basement and called for him to come upstairs. He told her to wait in the bathroom and leave if he didn't come back soon. She waited there for an hour before she let herself out.

"How did you get home?"

"I walked back to the Metro and got on the train."

"But after the Metro? You took the bus back?"

"I tried to. But the bus never came. I think, like, it was done for the night. I didn't realize they stopped."

"So what did you do?"

"A man drove by and told me he'd give me a ride home. He said he had a daughter and hoped someone would do the same for her one day. He said, like, he was paying it forward."

I was afraid to ask the next question. "So you got in the car?"

"Yeah," she said matter-of-factly. "I was far from my house."

I was truly dumbfounded by her choices. Chelsea and I looked at each other, wondering how this girl was still alive. I couldn't decide if she had angels or demons. "What happened when you got home?"

"I got back in bed."

"So, how did they find out? When did you tell them?"

"I didn't. My mom was checking my phone and she saw he was texting me about it, like how I felt."

"He wanted to know how you were feeling about it?" Chelsea asked.

"No. Like he was saying how I felt. Like that night. My mom freaked out and called my dad. And they called the police and stuff. And the school. They're Catholic. I mean, we're Catholic, so."

"What did you tell them happened?" I asked.

"I didn't really. I mean, they said what they think happened. Like I've been taken advantage of and stuff." She seemed less sure of herself now.

"Is that how you feel?"

She shook her head. "Not really. I just kind of thought it would be different."

"What would?"

"My first time."

Chelsea looked at me. "I see."

"So what's gonna happen to him? I mean, like, is he gonna get in a lot of trouble?"

I blinked at her. Even if he managed to escape jail time, he would likely be a registered sex offender for the rest of his life now. "Yes, he's in trouble," I said plainly.

She chewed on the inside of her lip. She shrugged her shoulders again. I wondered if she understood the gravity of the situation, both for her and him.

We heard a knock at the door. Her father stuck his head inside. "Everything okay? Just wanted to check on her. On you guys. Do you need us?"

"Just give us like two more minutes. I'll come right out and get you and then we can all talk."

"Sure, sure," he said. "Take your time. Thank you. We're just right outside, sweetheart."

Chelsea turned back to her. "I think you should tell your parents what really happened. All of it. Including how you left the house and almost didn't make it back. That was a stupid decision. You could've been killed."

She shrugged again and looked at me.

"No, she's right. I'm honestly surprised you would have gotten in the car with a stranger. And that's not even the reason we are meeting. You should tell your parents what really happened."

"What if I don't want to? Like, this conversation is privileged or something, right?"

"Well, I'm not exactly your attorney, and you're not exactly my client." I didn't elaborate. "But you should explain what really happened that night and how old you told him you were. We can help you figure out the best way but if this goes forward, there will be aspects we have to disclose."

"Fine. Okay. If it will make all this stop. I don't wanna be here. I'm sick of it. They're acting like I have cancer."

Chelsea stood to open the door and invite her parents inside.

They were already standing when she opened it. Their blank expressions convinced us they had not been listening. They sat next to her, flanking her on either side.

"I think your daughter has something to tell you," Chelsea said.

"Okay," her father said, turning to her. "Tell me what?" He and his wife looked at each other, wondering who knew what. They were holding hands. They looked at their daughter. "Tell us what, sweetheart?" her father said. "You can tell us anything. You know that."

She repeated the story, leaving out the part that she had brought the condom. We interjected intermittently to help her.

". . . and I got back in bed." Her mother sat back. Her father kept staring at her, twisting his body toward her but keeping his hands folded on the table.

After a beat, he remembered he had an audience. He smiled, letting it fade quickly as if it were a spasm. "Give us a minute. We will need a minute. Can we have a minute?"

"Yes, of course," I said. Chelsea and I stood up and put ourselves on the other side of the door.

"What the fuck?" Chelsea whispered.

"The poster child of an after-school special. You can't make this stuff up. What the hell?" I shook my head as we compared moments of disbelief.

He opened the door a few minutes later, beckoning us back in.

"Okay, we've decided what she wants to do." I noted his odd word choice. "We're going to go forward. He needs to be in jail. She didn't know what she was doing. You can't prove she lied about her age."

Out of sheer curiosity, I waited to see how much more he would try to dictate.

"No," Chelsea said. She didn't share my curiosity.

"Excuse me?" he said.

"No. We're unlikely to go forward with this case, but we'll let you know what we decide to do."

"You'll let me know? You'll let *me* know?" he repeated. "Do you have any idea how this makes me look? People know about this now. Because my *wife* called the school without talking to me first." His tender concern for his family quickly morphed into anger. His tone was no longer deliberately soothing; it was now more like a growl.

He clasped his hands together and tapped his index finger against his top lip. "If we don't go forward with this, with something. You know what it will look like. Like she is some tramp who didn't know the buses stop running at midnight." He smiled with a spasm again, struggling to contain his anger. "So, we would like to go forward. To press charges. I don't care which you want to . . . charge. But we will go forward. You will deal with him and I will— we will—deal with her."

"We'll evaluate the case thoroughly. We don't just bring charges to save face. It doesn't work like that, sir," I responded.

"Oh, I think it does. I think it will. Do you know who I am? Where I work?"

"Do you know where I work?" I held his gaze.

He smirked, exhaling like a punch as he put his hands in his pockets. "Come on." He turned to his wife, instructing her not to speak.

"It was nice to meet you. We will, we will be in touch with your boss."

"I'll tell him to expect your call. After I type out the notes of our conversation. Chelsea? Do you also need time to add your notes to the file?"

"I do," she said. "It won't take me long. I want to make sure I get the last part down verbatim before I forget."

"Well," he said. "Well," he repeated, guiding his daughter by the back of her arm as he retraced the few steps back to the elevators.

His daughter looked back at us. She rolled her eyes again.

Chelsea and I headed back to my office to postgame. Rebecca looked up as we passed, asking as we walked by, "Was I right?" I could hear her getting up to follow me down the hall, repeating, "Was I right?" We stopped to avoid the chase.

"Yup," Chelsea said, knowing the reaction we would get.

"Ha!" Rebecca said, clapping her hands. "I knew it!" She pointed at me like I was the accused. "I *knew* it! You see why I hate these cases. I never do them. I told you!" She was fully gratified by her coincidental clairvoyance here.

"She even lied about her age," Chelsea added.

Rebecca shook her head. "Yeah, but, see, that's why I hate these cases so much! Cuz it doesn't matter if he actually knew her age or not. It's ridiculous." She walked back toward her office, exclaiming a final time, "I was right!"

Chelsea and I looked at each other and the file she was still holding in her hand. We both knew one of us might now officially be assigned to this case. Chelsea playfully dropped the file on the ground in anticipatory refusal and shouted, "Not it!"

15

Chess Pie

On a Prosecutor Embraced Outside of the Courtroom

Traveling alone, I was in a small town somewhere in Mississippi. It was on the eve of an election, and as a trial attorney in the Civil Rights Division of the Department of Justice, I was assigned to monitor the polling places to ensure there were not violations of the Voting Rights Act. My team and I hadn't been able to coordinate our flights, and I was a day behind them. I hoped to meet up with them at a hotel we'd picked out. The Deep South made me nervous. Where I was heading, I'd be practically equidistant from the 16th Street Baptist Church that the KKK bombed, killing four young Black girls attending Sunday School; the home where veteran and civil rights activist Medgar Evers was assassinated; and the river in which two White men drowned fourteen-year-old Emmett Till. Warranted or not, it was impossible to see anything but duplicity in the White faces that smiled back at me.

I checked my gas tank three times before I left the airport. I charged my phone along a wall in the airport for thirty minutes before I left the gate.

Wanting to make sure I arrived near the hotel before sunset, I calculated that after the drive, I would have about an hour before nightfall set in. I watched for food signs along the highway where the restaurant was visible from the highway exit. I had learned long ago not to turn off a main road without seeing the destination. Exit after exit, the food signs directed me to a stop a few miles down the road. I kept driving. I had to stay on schedule to avoid looking for food near my hotel in the dark. Worst-case scenario, I figured, I'd find a drugstore and grab something to fill up on.

I neared the hotel with light still in the sky, so I decided to drive around to see if there was a restaurant anywhere in the vicinity. The plane ride had made me nauseous, and I preferred to eat something real. Besides, tomorrow would be an early start and I needed to have something in reserve in case I couldn't catch my breath before the polls closed the next evening. This might be my last chance at a good hot meal before the chaos of the vote tally.

A few blocks from the hotel, I passed a restaurant tucked along a square. I figured I'd eat alone quickly rather than try to coordinate a group dinner with the team. The street was busy, but there was a parking lot right out front. I pulled in, wondering if my plates were in-state. I only had a carry-on and wore my suit on the plane to avoid its getting wrinkled in the bag. I regretted not changing first as I surveyed the wardrobes of the passersby. I left my suit jacket clinging to the back of my headrest and grabbed my coat instead. I put it on as I looked up at the sign.

The restaurant seemed nice enough from the outside. I texted my father to let him know I'd arrived and the name of the restaurant. He called back instead of texting.

"Where are you now?"

"I'm about to go into the restaurant now . . . No, I'm alone for now, but there are others coming soon. I'll call you from my hotel room. I should be there in under an hour, I'm guessing . . . Oh no, it's close. Walking distance. Of course I didn't walk . . . Let me get off the phone as I walk in so I'm not that woman in the restaurant, okay?"

The bell over the door announced my entrance as I stepped inside.

Five patrons looked up from their plates and coffee cups and sized me up.

"Can I help you, ma'am?" a White waitress called out as she poured a cup of coffee for a customer.

"Just one," I said, indicating with my finger.

"Please seat yourself. Anywhere you like, ma'am. Take your pick," she said, gesturing at the empty tables.

There were four open tables, three of which were adjacent to diners who exchanged glances with one another as they tried not to draw attention to the empty seat beside them. I spotted a booth kitty-corner to a four-top with two diners.

"Alright if I take the booth along the wall?" I said, alleviating the suspense.

"That'd be fine. I'll be right with you, darling." She refilled another mug down the counter line before bringing a yellowed laminated menu to me. "You want to hear the special?"

I looked around, surprised there were specials. "Sure. What are your specials?"

"*The* special," she corrected me, "is meatloaf with a choice of two sides. Creamed corn, okra, coleslaw, or mashed potatoes with gravy." She held her pen close to the pad, ready to write the instructions to the cook.

"Thank you. I just need a minute."

"Take your time. What can I get you to drink?"

"I'll take a sweet tea, please. No ice."

"Okay, I'll get your drink and be right back to take your order, alright?" She never looked up until the last word.

From my vantage point, I could see the entire restaurant clear through to the front door. I had the impression that the restaurant had been louder when I'd walked in. I glanced around the room. I was the only Black person inside.

A man at the counter with rolled-up sleeves and a baseball hat twisted his stool toward me and stared while he sipped the coffee our waitress had just poured. He blew on the top before each sip. He lifted his cap slightly, not as a nod to chivalry but to allow me to see his eyes more clearly. He didn't turn away when our eyes met, if only out of embarrassment. He just sipped his coffee as he watched me.

I scanned the menu and tried to find whatever food would easily show if someone had tampered with it. Nothing with gravy, or sauce, or anything else that could cover someone's spit under a bun. Something fried, served so hot it would kill the bacteria, was always the best option.

President Obama had been in office for nearly two years at this point, but on trips like these I still wondered if someone would spit in my food. The tea was already in a pitcher on the counter when I walked in, so I could watch it being poured.

A refrigerated display case with sliced pie was in front of me, with dessert plates stacked beside it. The removal would be visible from where I sat. Dessert would be possible tonight as well.

The waitress returned with my tea, with a plate of sliced lemons and a straw atop a paper doily.

"I'm going to have the fried chicken with a side of greens and candied yams. Dark meat, if you have it."

"Alright, I'll put that right in," she said, tucking the menu under her arm.

"And what kind of pie is that in the case? Is that lemon meringue I see?"

She turned around to see where I was looking.

"No, ma'am, that's an icebox pie you're seeing. We also have a pecan pie and a chess pie left there, too."

"You make it here?"

"Yes, ma'am." She was still scribbling on her pad. I wondered how long it took to write out my order. She paused and looked at me. "Which one do you want?"

"I've never had a chess pie. I'll have that, too. Is it good?"

"If you like sweet," she said, still writing. She stopped writing to ask, "You want the pie now or after?"

"After, thank you."

"Okay. I'll put this right in."

She tore my order from her pad and placed it on the wheel ticket holder. She spun it back and called to a man in the kitchen. She repeated the order aloud, inexplicably. A Black man came into view, taking the ticket off the wheel.

He smiled with his eyes over the aluminum counter, and nodded as he said, "Coming right up."

I relaxed for a moment. I realized I could've had the gravy.

I picked up my phone and scrolled to distract myself, confirming the schedule for the next day. I started to map the distance from my hotel to the first polling site when the man at the counter spoke up.

"You ain't never had chess pie? Where you from?" He was still blowing over his coffee. It couldn't possibly be that hot.

"I'm not too big on sweets," I lied, drawing the conversation away from his question.

"Mmmmm." He slurped his coffee, exhaling after the gulp. "I've been trying to do better myself about that. But I've got one helluva sweet tooth."

"Is that right?" I said, returning to my phone.

"Oh yes, I could eat cakes and pies all day. Especially chess pie. These aren't like Ms. Shirley's, but she makes 'em alright." He pointed toward the waitress. I wondered who Ms. Shirley was.

"Well, then, I can't wait to try it." I returned to my phone.

"Where'd you say you were from, again?"

I hadn't. I weighed whether to answer. "Oh, today I'm just coming from Jackson." I tried to remember some of the landmarks I passed on the way from the airport, in case he asked.

"Jackson. I hear it's really changing."

"Oh, you know, the more things change, the more things stay the same."

"I could've sworn that was a rental car. It looks like one, doesn't it, Ray?"

I waited for Ray to respond so I could locate him. The man at a nearby four-top agreed, keeping his back to me.

"Where were you before today? When you come from Jackson?"

Being coy wasn't in my best interest, since being evasive raised too many red flags. I remembered I was alone and wanted to flex my muscle to feel safe.

"Washington, D.C. The Department of Justice. My team is here to monitor the elections. I might have to bring them back a slice of this pie tonight if it's as good as you say it is. They're waiting for me to meet them just as soon as I finish eating."

"Now why would the Department of *Justice* be here watching us? I've never heard of any problems. You heard of any problems, Ray?" he asked.

"No, sir," Ray answered, this time looking over his shoulder.

"You ever hear of any problems back there?" he shouted toward the cook's window.

The cook's eyes looked up and shot a glance in my direction. His shoulders moved as he plated a meal and rang the bell. He placed a to-go box in a plastic bag and looked at me for a moment.

"She didn't order this to go. She's eatin' in." The waitress raised her voice, irritated.

I looked at the cook. He trained his eyes on mine and rolled them toward the door. I interjected before she could speak again.

"Actually, I am gonna take it to go, after all. Everybody's waiting on me. I'll just take the check, if that's alright."

"You still want the pie? I already added it to your check."

"Sure, that's fine. I'll take that to go, too," I said, making my way to the register.

The man at the counter turned his stool as I passed. He blew on his coffee as I waited to pay.

"You wanted the chess pie still?" she asked.

"Yes, she hasn't had chess pie, right? Give her your best piece," the man at the counter said between slurps.

I watched as she opened the refrigerated case and pulled out the pie. She wiped a knife along a wet white towel folded underneath it. She turned the pie to put the missing slice off-center before she cut into the crispy brown crust on top, separating the slice from the rest of the pie. She slid the knife under the pie and placed her finger lightly on top to steady it as she swiftly moved it toward a plastic flip-top container. The restaurant was silent as she snapped the lid together at the corners.

"You want it inside the bag?"

"I'll just carry it separately."

She typed the amounts into the register and swiveled the monitor toward me to reveal the total.

She held out her hand for payment. I handed her my card and she swiped it along the machine.

"It might take a minute," she said, sitting on the stool as she waited. She slid the pie on the counter but held on to the bag as she waited for the approval notification.

"What exactly are you looking for, Ms. Justice Department?" he probed.

"Tell you the truth, right now I'm looking for a packet of hot sauce."

"Hot sauce was on the table, hon. We don't have it to go." The waitress smiled for the first time.

The man named Ray walked out of the restaurant.

"How many of you are there down here?" The man at the counter was relentless. "Where you gonna be? Just certain places, or everywhere?"

"Oh, we'll be around." The machine beeped an approval. "We all set? I left the tip on the table already."

I shot a glance back toward the cook. "Thank you," I said to him alone.

"Be careful now," he said. I wondered about the nature of his warning. I turned to see Ray's food half-eaten, his companion still sitting at the four-top awaiting his return.

I walked outside to a setting sun and into a cloud of smoke. Ray was smoking beside my rental car. I moved the bag and pie to one hand to free the other to unlock the car.

"You know where you're going?" he said, moving away from the car.

"Yyyyup," I said, opening the door and sitting down quickly. I locked the doors instinctively before putting on my seat belt. I looked up from the click to see Ray smiling.

I pulled out toward the hotel, my eyes peeled to the rearview mirror to see if any car was following me.

As I walked into the hotel, I threw the food away out of an abundance of caution. It was better to be hungry than sick. I checked into the hotel and listened to the rundown of amenities, asking, "Do you have breakfast?"

"Absolutely. It begins at six a.m., right across from the lobby," the hotel clerk offered with hospitable glee. "Anything else I can help you with tonight?"

"Have you ever heard of chess pie?"

"Yes, my grandmother used to make it all the time. Haven't had it in years, though. I'm not all that into sweets."

I texted my father to tell him I was safely inside my room.

"Did you eat?" he asked.

"Not yet. I'll find something. I'm not hungry. I'd rather sleep than eat right now."

I woke up the next morning with a jolt. A dream had startled me awake, but my mind wouldn't let me remember anything but the anxiety. My alarm wasn't due to go off for another twenty minutes. I lay there trying to get my bearings and finally got up. It was not yet dawn. I laid out my clothes and started the shower, stealing a glance in the mirror. My eyes were swollen, as if I'd been crying, but I didn't recall any sorrow. My heart raced again as the toothpaste foam bubbled in my mouth. I put on my shower cap and stood in the scalding shower, exhaling deeply.

My alarm went off as I rinsed and I hopped out to silence its blare, drying myself as I scrolled back through my messages to confirm that we were indeed supposed to meet in the lobby soon.

I unplugged the phone from the charger and wrapped the cord around its base, tossing it in my purse. I put on my coat, and when I went to fix the collar, I could still smell the fried food from the restaurant. My stomach panged, suddenly hungry. It was 5:45; the breakfast in the lobby wouldn't start for another fifteen minutes. Maybe they'd be early today.

I scanned my files to confirm my routes. I highlighted the priority polling locations and wondered in which order it might make sense to arrive. The borders between districts separating polling locations zigzagged nonsensically. Geometry wasn't the point; dilution of voting power was. And it had been successful.

I placed the file in my purse and turned on the bedside lamp in my room, setting the television on low so I wouldn't return to complete silence. I hooked the Do Not Disturb sign to the front-door handle and closed the door behind me lightly, to avoid waking nearby guests. I waited until I heard the click before checking the handle to make sure it didn't budge and then walked to the elevator. The hotel had only a few floors, but I didn't want to risk getting trapped in the stairs.

It was approaching 6:00, and an older Black woman was just hanging the tongs on the handle of the silver food buffet trays when I approached. "Good morning," I greeted her.

"Good morning!" she returned cheerfully. "Did you sleep well?"

"I'm not sure. Ask me around noon today," I said with a laugh.

"You have to have an early start today?" she asked, nodding toward my suit.

"Yes. I'm heading down to the polls today. The polls open at seven."

"You're here to vote?" she inquired.

"I'm actually monitoring the polls today. I'm with the Department of Justice. There are a few of us here today throughout the area."

"God is good . . ." She led with it as if it were a password.

"All the time," I finished. She smiled and motioned to where the plates were.

"Okay if I get started? This smells too good."

She chuckled. "I made it just for you, then. The waffle batter is on ice right there. The syrup is these little things right here. The eggs and grits and meat are inside these. Sausage links and bacon. I like my bacon crispier, but I've got to make it for everyone, so." She laughed.

I walked toward the cereal boxes.

"I thought you were hungry?" she said.

"Oh, I am, I'm taking one of these for the road. I'm definitely going to get a little bit of everything."

I sat when the weight of the Styrofoam plate began to give way, determined to eat enough to fuel me for the day. My partner, a young paralegal in her twenties, was late, and it gave me time to finish eating as I waited to dispatch the rest of the team. She emerged from the elevator in a suit, looking disheveled. I blamed it on the early morning hours. She looked uncomfortable in her clothing and told me how much she hated wearing a suit, lamenting why we couldn't observe elections in jeans instead of this skirt.

"At least I won't be too hot in pants," she said, looking at mine. "It will feel like I'm wearing shorts at least, right?"

She tugged at a skirt that hit above the knee, exposing her bare legs. Somehow I knew it'd be an issue. I didn't have to wait long to confirm my beliefs. Marlene, a White retiree in her seventies with a deep drawl, approached us at our first polling site, intent on letting me know the exact nature of her issue.

"You're from the government?" Marlene asked, looking my colleague up and down, her gaze finally resting on her legs.

"We are. Is there a place you'd like for us to stand so that we're not in your way?" I responded.

"Stand where you want, as long as you don't bother the voters. There are rules, you know."

"I do. We'll stay out of your way best we can, but I'd ask you to assist us when you can. Fair enough?"

She nodded. Then, turning her focus to my colleague standing at a distance from us as she tugged on her suit jacket and adjusted her glasses, she asked me, "What's she gonna be doing? I'm assuming you're in charge just by the way you're dressed."

"She'll be observing as well," I explained. "I will leave soon for other polling locations but will check back periodically. She'll remain longer at times."

A line was starting to form, and I motioned for my colleague to get in position.

Marlene had a bone to pick. "You know you oughta tell that girl how to dress. She's got her fat legs out like a prostitute. Didn't even bother to wear stockings, and you're telling me she's here to watch me? Looking like that. You had the good sense to cover your legs. And you look nice. But she don't look professional at all, now does she?"

"Thank you, ma'am, for your feedback. I'll be sure to let her know how you feel."

"I can tell her myself if you'd like. I'm not a woman to mince my words. You can ask anyone about me. They'll tell you that. I make sure of it."

"I have no doubt." And I didn't. "I have a separate focus. I'm sure you do as well today, and I'd hate for this conversation to stop you from getting what you need to get done."

"Yes, we'll be very busy. I've been doing this for ten years. Ever since I retired. Anyone has any questions, they can just come to me. I've never had any complaints so I don't even know why you're here." Marlene folded her arms across her chest, allowing her body to shake as her arms settled into position.

"I'm so glad to hear that. I'm sure today will be no different. Excuse me," I said moving away from her toward my colleague.

"She was giving you an earful. What'd she have to say?" I had no intention of telling her the part of the earful that would make her ears burn.

"Oh, she was telling me that I wouldn't find any problems under her watch. She takes her job very seriously."

"Well, that's good. At least she was nice about it."

"Humph. Yes, she's nice alright." My colleague cocked her head and twitched her eyebrows downward, wondering what was behind my tone. I moved on: "Any issues you're seeing yet?" I knew it was early.

Marlene watched us as we watched her team, continuing to scan my colleague's attire with haughty derision. She walked back over to me with her hands in her pockets.

"You know . . . ," she said, moving her hands to a folded position across her chest. As she spoke, her thumb rose to play with the cross dangling from her chain. ". . . I don't think you ever showed me some identification. You should have a badge or something. Being from the Department of Justice and everything, right? I still have doubts about that one."

"Of course. I'm happy to show it to you," I handed her my credentials and waited for her to comment.

"Okay," she said, flipping it over before handing it back to me. "You let me know if there's some kind of problem . . ."

"We will. Please do the same."

She continued, eager to get one last dig in. ". . . Or if you need a chair or something. I'd offer one to her but I'd hate to see her try to sit down in that skirt."

"We're used to standing. But thank you for your continued concern, Marlene."

She didn't like hearing me say her name, correcting me. "Everybody calls me Mrs. Walker around here. On account of my days teaching."

I stared back, unwilling to rephrase. "Thank you for letting me know."

She blinked. "Well, I'm very busy. You just let me know."

I stretched my lips along my teeth in a forced smile and squinted to suppress an eye roll.

With more than a dozen other sites to visit before the polls closed, I wondered how many more Mrs. Walkers I would encounter before lunch. And sure enough, by mid-afternoon, she'd become a cliché across six sites, and I was already exhausted by the sanctimony.

But for every Mrs. Walker in a majority-White district, there was a Mrs. Washington managing the majority-Black district, eager to shake my hand or offer a hug.

"Thank you for coming. We're doing the best we can, so you just tell me what I could do to make it better. We're glad you're here." "Mrs. Washington" would greet me with a smile and then introduce me down the line to the poll workers and instruct them unnecessarily to give me whatever I needed.

"We're on the up-and-up around here. You tell President Obama that we are on the up-and-up down here."

Requests to relay messages to President Obama were as frequent as were voters scanning their ballots. An air of inexplicable excitement spread, while a game of polling-place telephone transformed "We are monitoring the election" to "President Obama himself asked her to come." Even my insistence that his role be clarified was met with winks. People refused to detour from their perception. Instead, they acted like I had a secret and they were indulging me by keeping it. I kept my distance and focused on my task, nodding occasionally as poll workers pointed me out to incoming voters.

I was about to head out of one polling site when a Black man my father's age approached me. "There's someone I'd like you to meet."

He was ushering an old woman dressed in her Sunday best, complete with a lavender hat, by the elbow. She pressed her cane into the ground as she repositioned her leg between strides. She trained her eyes on mine as she walked. I walked to meet her where she was.

"Hello, ma'am. How are you?" I said, smiling, as she extended her warm, soft hand, contorted by arthritis. I clasped it between both of mine. She released her cane to the man who had introduced us, who must have been her son, placing her other hand on top of mine and squeezing. She shuffled closer, and I could instantly smell my own grandmother's hair cream. I wondered how old she was.

"You tell President Obama"—her words fired like a slow cannon as she patted the top of my hand with each syllable, lingering on the final word with a swallow—"that I voted for him and that he is making us proud. You tell him that I lived to see the day."

I indulged her willingly. "I sure will, ma'am."

"You tell him and those babies that we are prayerful. A Black man in the Oval Office. My God. We are prayerful."

"Yes, ma'am," I said, still holding her hands.

"My grandson brought me down here to vote today." I was dying to ask her age now. "And he told me that we had a Black woman, a sister, making sure no one messed with our votes."

I nodded.

"God bless you for coming. God bless President Obama for making it so. I always vote now. I always come out. Rain or shine. I'm here, isn't that right?" she said, turning to her grandson. She must have been in her nineties if he was her grandson.

"Yes. She wouldn't miss it. Means too much. She was on the front lines. Been on the front lines," he explained.

"Thank you for all that you have done, ma'am," I reassured her, genuinely aware of my indebtedness.

"Now you tell President Obama"—she raised her hand to point at me for emphasis—"to keep fighting. You keep fighting."

She signaled the end of our conversation with an emphatic nod and reached back for her cane. I realized the room had fallen silent.

"I'm so happy to have met you, ma'am. Thank you for introducing yourself. What is your name, ma'am?"

"My name is Shirley Washington."

"It was so nice to meet you, Mrs. Washington."

"Everybody calls me Ms. Shirley around here, on account of my baking."

I smiled, recalling the reference. "I hear you used to make a mean chess pie."

She straightened her back and beamed at the thought: President Obama had heard of her, too.

16

It Didn't Have to Happen to Me

On the Haunting Effect of Secondary Trauma

There are days when I am so grateful to have been a prosecutor. To have witnessed the relief of a victim no longer living in fear. To have heard the emotional release of a father who got justice for his son. To have seen the happy tears of a woman finally being heard or the smile return to a child's face as he finally, for the first time, feels safe. To have the ammunition to challenge the mistruths that are fed to the masses in the name of equal protection under the law. There is an unparalleled adrenaline rush in eliciting truth from the most deceitful person or in conceiving of and executing a strategy that leads a jury to water and compels them to drink. There is no feeling like being the bold, unapologetic voice that siphons power from abusers to the abused and convicts them with their own lies.

But there are also days when I wish I had never left the comfort of private practice to embark on the journey of public service. Strangely, it's the only thing in my life I've ever lamented becoming expert at. The more practiced I became, the less the defendant had a chance of building a meaningful defense. My skill created an inaccessibility to justice that I couldn't countenance.

At times the collective memories of trauma are so overwhelming that I fear I might lose myself if I don't fill my time. The violence didn't happen to me. But it didn't have to. It eviscerated me nonetheless, and I still grapple with the scars of the secondary trauma. It seems to be an emotional indebtedness that I'm unable to pay.

Those are the days when I wish I could see justice through the rose-colored glasses of my own youth, and the idealism and naivete I brought as a righteous law student. That I could return to a time when I believed that justice was binary, achievable, and universally understood. I long for the days when I could examine injustice through the esoteric volleys of a classroom debate, when I didn't see the victim looking into my eyes as she placed her last seed of hope in my hands. The days when the memories didn't consume my subconscious, bursting to the surface without warning, arresting me mid-stride.

I underestimated the toll that constant human misery would take on my soul. I thought I'd be able to distance myself to avoid its becoming at times debilitating; that pursuing justice would help balance out people's suffering. But that distance doesn't stay distant, despite my best efforts to suppress the memories. I'll be walking through the grocery store with my daughter and see Goldfish crackers on the shelf, and I'll remember the way a defendant would use it to reward a child who kept her own abuse a secret. I walk past a homeless woman and I wonder if she's the one who was violently raped by the man who had just been released from prison. The one who screamed outside of a police station for six hours before someone let her inside. The one who the medical examiner said might contaminate the rape kit with her filth. The specimen they extracted led to the man's conviction, but they released her back onto the street without addressing the mental health issues that were undoubtedly exacerbated by her continued trauma. I think I see her from time to time, shouting into a wall, and I wonder if there's a new reason for her to scream.

When my children are running around the playground, I watch a man with a young girl and try to sort out if they're related, if she's comfortable, if she feels safe? I call my children over to hug them, staring over their shoulders, wondering if the defendants I put away are lying in wait to be released, resentful of the time they think I caused them to miss with their own children.

After my children misbehave and I verbally discipline them, I have to retreat to my closet to try to stop myself from imagining the fear on their faces exaggerated to match that of the child whose parents' rage saw no bounds. I battle with my children to eat, afraid to cede to their stubborn palettes but equally afraid of fully recalling a nutritional standoff that led to one stepfather's starving a boy in his bathtub, his ten-year-old body reduced to that of a child half his age. I close my eyes, reorienting myself, reminding myself that this didn't happen to your children. That's not what's happening here. You aren't that mother. You would never hurt your child. Six years later, I still have these conversations with myself.

I thought I had trained myself to experience pain without feeling it. When I was a child, my father would often invite me to watch a movie beyond my intellectual comprehension. He is a man with such depth of emotion that he is often transfixed by stories about the human experience of the most vulnerable among us. I would settle down cross-legged on the couch beside him as the scene unfolded, gasping with hysterical laughter or being reduced to tears. My parents and sisters would exchange incredulous glances at my dramatic reaction as they visually drew straws: Who was going to console the baby this time? I have cried while watching a kung fu movie. As a child. I've been carried out of more than one movie theater. As an adult.

Still, my father was unrelenting in his quest to expose me to the world and all that it had to offer. Whether it was a song about a terminally ill girl who thought she could save her life by making one thousand origami cranes, or "Strange Fruit" crooned eerily over a melody, or O. Henry's tale of the last leaf falling, or the indignity of the antebellum South captured by an artist's paintbrush, he showed me the world through the safe lens of art and literature and film. Inevitably I would cry—and I've realized, as an adult, that there was a method to my father's madness in exposing a child with my emotional proclivities to these influences, so that I could bear witness to tragedy. Or rather a pedagogy to his parenting—he was teaching me emotional resilience through vicarious experience.

"Laura, you've got to harden up. The world will eat you alive if you don't understand it. You've got to learn to train your mind to process what you feel and see. Appreciate the experiences without letting them consume you. And if you're lucky, you will have learned a painful lesson without personally having had to experience the pain. But more often than not, Laura, you will feel joy!" he would tell me. And he was right, partially.

A part of me resented my well of emotions, and others' ability to feel something without being consumed by it. How could we have seen the same thing and yet their responses could be as muted as mine were paralyzing, I wondered. I concluded that compartmentalization was the answer, so I learned to compartmentalize.

I learned to compartmentalize for emotional survival. I still allowed myself to feel, and deeply, but I couldn't allow it to affect me. I barricaded my soul with impenetrable armor to protect my sanity. You could move me, but I could not be harmed. Doing so dulled my reaction, not my emotion, and it heightened my intellectual passion. I learned to filter information, dispensing with the sentiment in favor of the solution. I learned to process my observations with a focused empathy—concerned about how that experience made that person feel instead of a selfish concern for how it made *me* feel hearing it. It didn't leave me apathetic to problems;

it made me ambitious to solve them. It's a quality that served me well professionally—the compartmentalization gave me intellectual distance; the distance gave me emotional clarity.

When I prosecuted cases, I dove into them with a vengeance. I voraciously consumed the evidence, meticulously combing through police files and evidence as I did my favorite movies, memorizing every line, each word part of a screenplay playing out in my mind. I even cast the roles. I imagined what it was like for the victim, and approached my evidentiary shortcomings with the healthy skepticism of an eager audience waiting to feel. And eager as I was to script the trial, I refused to let it penetrate my armor.

Some days, my armor needed reinforcement, my spirit needed rejuvenation. I found solace in my mother's biblical paraphrase: Get out from among them and hear your voice. I would walk outside, putting physical distance between my body and the pain that the courthouse symbolized. The change of scenery offered an emotional reprieve from the weight of responsibility. I would return recharged, with renewed resolve to focus, to advocate, to strategize, to convict in the name of justice. I would convert a bench in a Smithsonian museum into my office, and I would strategize on my blank canvas with the impressionists as my backdrop.

Little did I know that becoming a mother would make it impossible for me to see a blank canvas anymore. Despite my better judgment and honed compartmentalizing skills, my mind cast my own children in the role of the victims in each case. It was their voices I heard, their screams I elicited as testimony, the physical violence superimposed on their tiny bodies. It created an Achilles' heel that was a channel through which uncompartmentalized emotion could enter. I could not detach. It changed the way I viewed the cases, the defendants, the pursuit of justice. It changed the order of my prioritized allegiance.

I still remember the first moment when I could no longer detach, when I awoke to my son's cry in the middle of the night. He screamed with such ferocity and for such a duration that his lungs seemed to quiver at the end of each wail. It startled me so much that I fell off the bed trying to rush to him. I nursed him back to sleep but then endured a panic attack for the rest of the night. I tortured myself, believing that was the sound the infant-victim made when, well, when. My husband held me as I sobbed on his chest, as he tried to soothe me, repeating that our son was safe, that all babies cry, that I'd get used to it. He didn't understand what about this cry, as opposed to all the others, had triggered me. I couldn't explain.

I thought this trigger would be temporary, lasting until my child could explain the source of his tears. But it wasn't, and in fact intensified—his cries that were specific pleas for protection, for salvation, brought me to my knees.

Being a mother contextualized pain for me, transported me into the shoes of other mothers and their children. My own children were thrust into the stories of injustice I had previously compartmentalized and viewed from an emotional distance. Now instead they were in my lap, cradled in my arms, as I imagined what might happen to my own children out in the world. I started to hear my son cry and wondered if it was like the sounds that a young, savagely beaten Emmett Till made as he was forced to lift a seventy-five-pound fan into the back of a pickup truck, forced to load his own anvil of death that would be tied to his body as he was thrown into the river. I hear my son scream for me and I can feel the water coming in, suffocating me as I try to breathe. I fight back tears as I imagine what those last moments were like for him. Did he protest? Did he understand what they were going to do to him, or did he hope that humanity would enter their hearts and see a child begging for his life?

I choose to believe that God takes you before your body endures physical torture. That Emmett left this earth before his body was yanked from his bed. It is the only salvation for my psyche; the only way to understand the horrific nature of what he must have endured. It is the only battle in which I allow my heart to win out over my mind. Because if I am wrong, and a human being felt each blow, enduring each millisecond of terror as if it were an hour, I would lose my mind. I would lose my will to love all people, and my heart would be relegated to a simple muscle.

But being a prosecutor tormented that belief. My victims were alive, often having endured torture at the hands of an abuser they trusted, which made me question what happens to those who survive. Where do their minds go when God doesn't take them? What happens to their minds when they see the people who couldn't save them or, worse, the people who chose not to? What happens to their souls when they live to tell about the moment their appeals to humanity were rebuffed, their request for dignity spurned? What happens when their memories were not experienced vicariously but actually lived.

I know Emmett is not my son. And yet I can't tell you how many times I have thought about his death when I have looked at my own son. How many times I have replayed what it would have been like for him in that moment. What my son would have done. How he would have tried to explain. How he would have looked to see if I or anyone was coming down the road to save him, knowing I would be too far to help. Did maternal intuition rouse his mother from her sleep that night all the way in Chicago, creating a sense of foreboding and fear that she would later recall as the moment her son screamed for her to save him? Would my own intuition alert me in time to be that savior for my own child? The open casket his mother implored the world to view is still on display. With every

241

mother's child dying in plain view at the hands of those who ignore our appeals to humanity, I fear I might be woefully unprepared to endure what the world will do to my boy. How it will treat him when he makes a mistake. How it will hurt him. How it will make him carry his own anvils and deride him for not moving fast enough. What allegiances would be battling within the person that judges him in any arena?

I was scared when my mother told me that motherhood would be like watching your heart walk outside of your body for the rest of your life. I questioned whether I'd be strong enough to watch it roam in a country whose laws had unapologetically constricted the aortas of Black boys until they collapsed.

As I write, my shirt is soaked from the tears pouring from my eyes. I wonder even now if I am strong enough. If I will ever be. Morning will be here soon, and my children will need me. I know I better close my eyes, but my eyelids will not descend into slumber. I go to my son instead, to ensure that his eyelids indeed have. I tiptoe to his bedroom and stand at his doorway, watching to see if his comforter rises and falls with his breath. I move closer to see his face. It is calm, angelic in the glow of the middle of the night streaming through a segment of the blind that refuses to lay flat. He swallows and opens his mouth as he exhales, as if he knows he is safe. I wonder if he knows I'm close. I kiss his face, whisper the same thing I always do: "Mommy loves you. You are safe." He exhales again as his body turns away from the light, and I return to lie beside my husband. He looks like his son. And tonight, he is safe. I touch my belly, and whisper good night to my daughter.

"I love you, little girl. You are safe." I fall asleep imagining the sound of her voice and what might make her smile.

With a start, my eyes open just before dawn, my heart racing from a dream I can't remember but that has left me disoriented.

I am alone in the moment. I get out of bed, to place distance between myself and the pillow to avoid remembering what jolted me
awake. I wander around the house, lost, trying to understand my
emotions.

I stand.

I walk.

I fear.

I confront.

I recover.

I repent.

I hurt.

I heal.

I cleanse.

I regress.

I feel.

I am numb.

I remember.

I forget.

I care.

I disengage.

I analyze.

I process.

I reject.

I accept.

I compartmentalize.

I distinguish.

I cry.

I stop.

I ache.

I smile.

I boast.

I retreat.

I wish.

I lament.

I hope.

I regret.

I toil.

I thrive.

I continue.

I engage.

I falter.

I crave.

I fall.

I live.

I die.

I question.

I forgive.

I resist.

I flee.

I need.

I ask.

I don't.

I will.

I did.

I can't.

I reason.

I blame.

I debate.

I resolve.

I envy.

I believe.

I pray.

I rebuke.

I give.

I withhold.

I surrender.

I sleep.

I wake.

I push.

I share.

I recoil.

I explain.

I step forward.

I step back.

I speak.

I write.

Conclusion

Justice is an ecosystem, as complex as it is interconnected with those at its helm and at its mercy. Yet so many of our conversations around reforming the justice system center on how to prevent people from entering the system, rather than taking a holistic approach that considers those already within it. Officers and suspects, unions and legislators, heroes and villains, victims and assailants. These stories offer but a glimpse into what I was carrying within me, both figuratively and literally, in my pursuit of justice. The battles raging within are but a microcosm of the problem of defining and achieving justice in the midst of an ongoing racial reckoning. And that reckoning can't be dismissed as a response to a single police encounter.

Race permeates our entire justice system and informs how we even define what justice is—and who it's for. I've grappled with my many and competing allegiances, but there will be those who believe that my race is the only lens through which I evaluate and define justice. This is binary thinking: people tend to think that the opposition is on one side of the criminal justice system—on the side of either the defendants or the police.

For those who think that oppression wears the color blue, in my experience, there is great diversity among officers in terms of fairness, race, intellect, and personality. Not surprising, since they are, after all, human beings. While the overwhelming majority of officers I worked with served honorably, there were those drunk on power who abused their authority either physically or, perhaps more dangerously, through manipulation of the rule of law, exploiting the fact that while most people can recite the Miranda warning, they really have no idea what their rights are.

Where does this power come from? The gun? The badge? Reputation? No. The police force gets its power from case law, or precedent. Officers have a script. They are often better versed in the law than you can imagine. They can recite Supreme Court opinions that favor them as easily as my children recite the alphabet. They know precisely what to say to prove your guilt and to confirm they are acting appropriately even when they're not.

Nowhere is this more apparent than in cases of excessive force. Protesters and the media have focused on the obvious similarities between certain high-profile cases. I see the similarities with my eyes but also understand another layer of what's happening. When I use only my ears, what I hear is appalling: what each of these cases has in common is an officer reciting a script to avoid a charge of excessive force or murder. And it's working. The Supreme Court, in cases, has given officers a get-out-of-jail-free card. The courts have decided that because officers confront extremely dangerous scenarios and have to make split-second decisions under circumstances that the average person doesn't, we can't question their decisions. We have to defer to police officers and rely on their discretion— trust that only they know what they should have done. The courts use a "reasonable officer" standard, meaning that they will judge that officer against what another reasonable officer would have done. A self-interested jury of their peers. The only way to change this standard—and it should absolutely be changed to "reasonable person," not simply reasonable officer—is to have the Supreme

Court rule again (and that ain't happening anytime soon) or have legislation that changes the standard. If you want to change the law, you've got to make a law.

If you think that the carte blanche we give officers to exercise their discretion is not a big deal, consider this: we give officers that same deference for arrests. You are innocent until proven guilty in a court of law, right? That presumption of innocence that we all hold so dear only matters when you get to trial. Getting to trial is an up-hill battle. Once an officer arrests you, and the prosecutor decides to charge you with the crime the officer said you committed, you are at the mercy of the court to give you access to that presumption of innocence. How can that be? It's a little word that carries a big stick: bail.

The purpose of bail is to ensure that you show up to future court proceedings. If you miss the court hearing, then you risk forfeiting your money. If you even have the money to post it. Courts often set staggering bail to ensure a defendant shows up, dollar amounts reaching into the tens and hundreds of thousands. Most people simply cannot afford to pay such high amounts. Instead, these defendants rely on bail bondsmen for a loan with predatory interest rates, where such services are even available. For a nonrefundable fee of 10 percent of the bail amount, the bail bondsmen will loan a defendant the money to pay bail. For many, the choice is clear: pay a bail bondsman or wait in jail for trial. For many others, the choice is illusory when you don't even have access to the 10 percent.

None of this is coincidental. Centuries of social and economic inequity have created a domino effect. Systemic and sanctioned racism leads to racial profiling, which leads to higher incidents of arrest. Arrests lead to bail requirements. Failure to meet that requirement leads to incarceration pending trial. Incarceration pending trial leads to an increased likelihood of psychological deterioration and a decreased ability to mount a strong defense, which leads to higher rates of conviction. Even if you are released, the record of arrest or conviction leads to further economic disadvantage. Both arrests and convictions factor into the court's calculus in deciding what your bail will be. The more prior arrests you have, the higher the bail is often set.

If you are offered a plea to avoid this, you must act quickly, so that the initial plea offer doesn't expire, only to be replaced with one far more punitive as you approach trial. Defense counsel knows this and advises clients of what is in store for those who can't afford bail: remain caged and hope to convince twelve people of your innocence, or take the plea and convince one judge to be lenient at sentencing. Pressure is on defendants to plead guilty to a crime they may or may not have committed, simply because they can't afford to do otherwise. Misjudge the jury or choose the plea and you have a conviction that weighs against your release. Damned if you do. Damned if you don't.

We need reform. While we need peaceful protest as a response to the ills you see, now is the time for legal architecture. As a prosecutor, I never had the luxury of wearing sociological blinders, and I never wanted to. We have to demand that our courts and congresspeople don't wear them, either. Race prominently stands at every intersection in America. It shapes our legal policy, our charging decisions.

Just look at the how we select a jury. While the intent is to provide defendants with a jury of their peers, "peer" is loosely defined. It doesn't require that you have jurors of the same race, gender, or religion as the defendant, or from the same neighborhood. It merely requires that the jurors be randomly selected by a group of people living in the same city. From among those randomly selected for jury duty, the pool is whittled down during voir dire, further reducing the likelihood that the jury will resemble you. While the law requires justice to be blind, the law also recognizes that lawyers have perfect vision. When lawyers select jurors through the voir dire process, they are required to write down the race of the juror they wish to strike. Why? Because it is in jury selection that lawyers attempt to gain the advantage for defendants or stack the deck against them, with race being the presumptive unifying or dividing factor. Case law requires the judge to ensure that jurors are not struck on racial grounds, so if the striking decisions of either attorney suggest an inappropriate pattern, the attorney is required to justify the strike on non-racial grounds. And it had better be good, or you will risk losing your license to practice law. The unintended consequence of color-blind jury selection? It becomes a primary focus. The inner dialogue goes something like this: "That person is awful for our case. But, dammit, I already struck three White women in a row. It will look suspicious if I strike another. I better strike someone else. Watch, that juror is going to be the holdout."

Race matters at trial. A juror's job is to assess credibility. The juror observes the demeanor, dialect, mannerisms, and attire of the witnesses and decides whom to believe. Every cultural idiosyncrasy and stereotype is on full display for the world to see and judge. Human nature requires that people like those with whom they can identify. In addition to the facts, jurors decide cases on whether they see themselves in the defendant or the victim. What would I have done had I been in his or her shoes? Whomever the jury humanizes more wins. Understandably, a person's race factors into that calculation.

Race matters at sentencing. The judge considers the defendant's personal history, criminal record, if any, mental health, community experience. Race permeates all of that.

Race even informs your objectivity. Objectivity is learned as much as it evolves. It is not innate. Objectivity is the culmination of experience, regret, and empathy. To be objective, one must have challenged the absurdity or sanctity of one's own beliefs. Objectivity is accelerated by having your nose rubbed in your own mistakes and your flaws inconveniently revealed. It comes from having your naive viewpoints tested and your intellect belittled. It stems from being the victim of condescension and the one in the position to condescend. And it comes from your own victimization and what you do when you have the choice to victimize. Amid those epiphanies, objectivity emerges.

My race always informed my objectivity. I know what it is like to be mistaken for less than I am because of the way that I look. America doesn't assume that every White person is a hillbilly with little educational attainment, poor values, and an extensive criminal history. No, the embodiment of that stereotype is merely the cringeworthy exception, and race is coincidental. But Black people are preemptively judged by the most unflattering depictions of our race, even if the depiction is fictionalized. The presumption is that the stereotype and its embodiment are so pervasive that if a person does not conform, they are the exception. Despite the overwhelming truth that the depraved uneducated criminal with a demonstrated indifference to society is the exception, the lie prevails.

It is precisely because I am a Black woman that the blackness of a defendant was never an indictment. It didn't preclude my ability to draw a distinction between myself and a defendant. I understood our relative positions in the courtroom, and I understood the depth of diversity within my race. The diverse personal journeys and values, the strength of social conscience, the contribution made to the world. In the pursuit of justice, I prosecuted the content, even when the character looked like me.

Race informs your patriotism. It is impossible to evaluate America in a vacuum. Holding your hand to your heart while you pledge allegiance to a symbol and to a country that has gone to great lengths to tell you what it thinks of your race and gender, attempting to silence your mind during the singing of the national anthem—these, too, are virtually impossible. Your mind replays pain as readily as it replays pride.

Race informs your sense of justice. Justice is not so easily defined. In fact, it's not at all what you think. It's a cost-benefit analysis: a compromise that yields no true satisfaction because it can't reverse the loss or suppress the memory of the wrong. But it begins the process of healing. It is a recognition of an injustice, validation of your feelings through collective grievance, an affirmation that you or someone you love matters, a punitive consequence, and a morsel of hope that the one who wronged you so will be denied the opportunity to be either oblivious to or dismissive of your pain.

And perhaps that's where the story begins.

Acknowledgments

The process of writing a book is like climbing the stairs of a high-rise with forty-seven flights. With each step you feel the weight of isolation a solo project requires. When you reach the top, or in this case the completed work, you should take a moment, catch your breath, look around, and recognize how you got there. It only takes a moment to discern that at each stage of progress, there was someone or something to motivate you.

There were those who provided the inspiration and facility to get you started. Others who contributed directly and indirectly as you passed each level along the way. And equally important, others who were present to cheer and support you while providing you with the sustenance to continue.

My attempt to express my gratitude to all of the above will fall short I am sure. There will never be enough words to state how much I appreciated all of your active contributions. But I will take several steps in that direction anyway.

I want to first thank my husband, Dale, for always believing in me, walking beside me, and understanding me. I respect and love you completely.

Next, I want to thank my incredible children for the immeasurable joy they exude and bring. It's an honor to be your mother, and

ACKNOWLEDGMENTS

I am now and will always be proud of you both. You make me want
to be better.

I have an amazing family. They have provided a loving and encouraging base not only for this project but for every stage of my
life. To my parents, Norman and Martha, I love and revere you with
all that I am, have been, and will be. Thank you for your example,
resilience, and unconditional love, respect, guidance, and support.
And to my big sisters, Tracey and Jennifer: our bond is unbreak-
able and we alone will remember the moments that made us who
we are. You are my teachers and heroes, and I will always look up
to you.

Then there's the family I chose, my dearest friends. Each of you
know what you mean to me. Thank you especially to Steven Wright,
an incredible friend and extraordinary writer whose mentorship has
been invaluable throughout this process.

Of course, there wouldn't be a book without the incredibly tal-
ented team at Simon & Schuster, including Dana Canedy and Steph-
anie Frerich; and my UTA family, Jerry Silbowitz, Pilar Queen, and
Mary Pender. You understood my vision of what I felt this book
could be. You were each in my corner, encouraging me to speak my
truth. I am proud of what we have accomplished.

I'm also extremely grateful to Emily Simonson, Navorn John-
son, Lewelin Polanco, Beth Maglione, Kimberly Goldstein, Alison
Forner, Christopher Lin, Julia Prosser, Cat Boyd, and Stephen Bed-
ford, who worked on the mechanics of making this book and sharing
it with the world. I thank each of you for your vision and tenacity.

To all of my mentors and colleagues, you have been integral
parts in making this vision of ours become a reality. I thank you
from the bottom of my heart.

Finally, let me say that the stories told in this missive are about
real human beings, as am I. Throughout my career in the Justice

ACKNOWLEDGMENTS

Department my role was to be a prosecutor and not a judge. I did not try to judge the participants then, nor will I now.

I would like to think that I leaned into my fate, and allowed my faith to guide me.

I thank all those dedicated men and women in law enforcement, the Department of Justice, and those whose lives I may have touched and have touched mine in a positive way. May we all continue in our just pursuits.

About the Author

Laura Coates is a CNN anchor and senior legal analyst and a SiriusXM host. A former federal prosecutor, Coates served as Assistant United States Attorney for the District of Columbia and a trial attorney in the Civil Rights Division of the Department of Justice, specializing in the enforcement of voting rights throughout the United States. As a civil rights attorney, she traveled throughout the nation supervising local and national elections and led investigations into allegations of unconstitutional voting practices. In private practice, Laura was an intellectual property litigator with an expertise in First Amendment and media law. A graduate of Princeton University's School of Public and International Affairs and the University of Minnesota Law School, Coates resides outside of Washington, D.C., with her husband and two children.